STRUCTURING PLAY IN THE EARLY YEARS AT SCHOOL

SCHOOLS COUNCIL PROJECT
THE STRUCTURING OF PLAY IN THE INFANT/FIRST
SCHOOL

Structuring Play in the Early Years at School

Kathleen Manning and Ann Sharp

Ward Lock Educational
in association with
Drake Educational Associates

The Structuring of Play in the Infant/First School

This Schools Council Project is based at the University of Sussex where it is working from 1974–8.

Project Team members

Co-Directors	Miss Kathleen Manning
	Mrs Ann Sharp
Project Officer	Miss Angela Baker
Project Officer/	
Evaluator	Miss Ann Ternouth

ISBN 0 7062 3602 5 paperback

First published 1977
Reprinted 1978, 1979, 1980, 1983, 1986

Set in 11 on 12 point Monotype Imprint
and printed in Hong Kong
for Ward Lock Educational
A Ling Kee Company
47 Marylebone Lane, London W1M 6AX and
Drake Educational Associates
212 Whitchurch Road, Cardiff CF4 3XF

Contents

Part 3 The teacher and play

Illustrations by Priscilla Lamont
Photographs and cover photograph by Educational Development
Services, The Polytechnic of North London, shot at Goldfield Infants
School, Tring

Preface

Structuring Play in the Early Years at School is a book for infant teachers and all those who wish to take a fresh look at the use of play as a teaching medium and its importance in infant and first schools. It is written as a reference and resource book for teachers and all concerned with the education of young children. It can be used by individual teachers working on their own, or as the basis for group workshops meeting in schools or teachers' centres. It is based on the work of six hundred teachers who took part in the Schools Council Project on the Structuring of Play in the Infant and First School. The book, in consequence, has a practical approach and will be of use to all infant teachers, no matter where they are or in what circumstances they find themselves.

The overwhelming majority of the teachers involved in the Project were women and in order to avoid confusion we refer to the teacher in feminine terms throughout the book.

We wish to acknowledge our debt and record our thanks to all the teachers who worked with us: without their help and cooperation the Project could not have taken place.

The need behind the Project

The idea of the Project first arose because of the difficulties which many teachers were experiencing in using play in the classroom. Although accepting that children learn and develop through play and that play is a motivating force for children's learning, many teachers are pressurized by the very full first school curriculum and large classes to neglect play as a means of teaching. They leave children to play on their own. In addition, many parents' expectations are that children will 'work' when they come to school, not 'play'; to quote Piaget (1969), 'Play is . . . neglected because it appears to be devoid of functional significance . . . no more than a form of relaxation.' Parry and Archer (1975) in their book *Two to Five* highlighted two ways in

7

which play can be used – 'One merely keeps children occupied: the other contributes to their educational development.' We found that teachers wanted help to integrate children's learning activities through self-motivated play and in this way integrate the learning of specialized 'subjects'. There is a danger, which many teachers appreciate, that if children learn separate groups of facts they may be unable to connect them because the central core of play-developed language and ideas has never grown. Thus children can only solve problems in isolation and fail to see the reality of their relevance to other similar situations.

Setting up the Project

The Project on Structuring Play was therefore set up to look at play in the infant classroom and to produce materials which would help teachers to structure play in school so that learning and development would take place.

The Project started in September 1974 with a grant from the Schools Council initially for three years' work. It was based in the Education Area at the University of Sussex. Twenty-seven working parties of teachers, each led by a liaison officer, were organized throughout England and Wales. The teachers worked for four terms with the Project. In the first stage they observed and recorded play in their classrooms: their records were used by the team to develop trial guidelines and video-tapes which were tried out by the teachers during the Project's second stage. This book embodies the work of the first and second stages. It is based on the observations and experience of teachers working with five to eight year olds in infant schools, first schools and all-age primary schools who volunteered to join the Project. The buildings they worked in ranged from board schools to modern open plan in rural, city and suburban areas. Classes numbered from less than twenty to over forty; the children came from every type of home background and covered all levels of ability. The teachers varied from young probationers to experienced staff nearing retirement.

Objective

The objective of this book, in conjunction with the Project's video-tapes, is to focus teachers' attention on the play opportunities that they are providing in their own classrooms and to make suggestions on the ways play can be developed. It also shows that if teachers take the cues from the children, play can motivate much of the learning and development in an infant class. The book can be used by teachers, whether they provide for play throughout the day, for half a day, or for set periods once or twice a week. *It does not suggest that children will 'pick up' the skills of reading and writing, nor that numeracy is acquired by chance in their play. These skills need to be taught by a teacher.*

We try not to repeat what can be found in related publications, for example those resulting from the Projects on Science 5–13, Communication Skills in Early Childhood, and Early Mathematical Experiences. But the teacher will find herself unable to develop play in her classroom or to answer the questions children ask in their play without reference to specialist publications.

Part 1 outlines the background to using play in school. Part 2 describes different kinds of play in the classroom, analyses their learning and development, and shows how they are structured by the teacher's observation, provision and involvement. Part 3 helps the teacher examine her own ideas and practice on the subject of play.

Making use of the Project materials

The book has been written to enable the teacher who reads it carefully to carry out the practical suggestions in the same way as the teachers in the Project. It can be used by teachers on their own but will more usefully form a basis for group work and discussion. The groups could be from one or more schools meeting in school or at a teachers' centre.

A set of video-tapes has been made which illustrates the kinds of play in the book. These give examples of children playing, of adult involvement, and show some of the learning and development that can occur in play. Suggestions on how to use the tapes for discussion and on organizing courses are contained in a booklet accompanying the tapes.

Play descriptions to analyse, suggestions for practical work in the classroom, and questions for discussion are provided throughout the book. An outline of further reading can be found in Appendix 2.

Teachers working with the Project found the group meetings invaluable in helping them to understand children's play, to analyse it carefully and to appreciate the adult's role in play. But it must be stressed that benefit will only accrue if teachers are willing to work systematically through the book, relate it to their own classroom situations and allow time for the play to develop. It is important not to expect immediate 'results'.

PART 1

Play in the infant school

1 Play and children's learning and development

The Project was based on the premises that children learn and develop through play, that play is a motivating factor for learning, and that adult help and participation are necessary for learning to progress.

Modern psychology is agreed that play is the starting point for cognitive development in the infant child (Isaacs 1930, 1933; Piaget 1951; Bruner 1966; Smilansky 1968; Furth and Wachs 1974). It is argued that discovery, reasoning and thought grow out of children's spontaneous activity; this may take the form of bodily skills and movement, make-believe play, or direct concern with physical things, animals and plants, and direct enquiry into whys and wherefores. Children learn by active and direct participation in concrete situations where the basis of problem solving and creative thinking is laid: 'The ability to evoke the past in play is very closely connected with the power to evoke the future in constructive hypothesis and to develop the consequences of "ifs"' (Isaacs 1930).

Play builds a bridge by which children can pass from the symbolic values of things to active enquiry into their real construction and real way of working: 'In play children gradually develop concepts of causal relationships, the power to discriminate, to make judgments, to analyse and synthesize, to imagine and to formulate' (DES 1967).

Also in play children experience the 'joy of being the cause' (Isaacs 1930) and will therefore sustain their activity to a satisfactory conclusion and develop the power to concentrate. There is no division between play and work in the infant mind: whatever he is doing, he is learning. His so-called playing is in fact working; he concentrates all his faculties on the one activity in which he is whole-heartedly engaged. It is this concentration that 'teaching-play' can exploit.

Cognitive learning includes the forming of concepts – mathematical and scientific, the use of language, the development of perception, investigation, exploration, imagination, experiment, problem solving, reasoning. When a young child is learning he will seldom be engaged in only one of these. For example, in establishing a mathematical or scientific concept he often practises his use of language and acquires a new vocabulary, or when investigating a new material he is led to explore a problem and to reason as he works out the solution. An imaginative idea leads to exploration as exploration may spark off an imaginative idea.

Play has this same quality; a make-believe play situation can cause children to experiment and question. For example, when playing a war game with boats in the water trough, boys discover that the boats do not always sink when they are 'bombed'. They try dropping different objects as bombs to see which are most effective. They drop the bombs from different heights to discover if this makes a difference. Similarly, exploratory play can spark off make-believe play. Two girls were experimenting with funnels and plastic tubing in the water tray. They discovered how the water flows through the tubing, watched it enter a funnel, clinging to the underside and dropping from the rim. They likened the water to a shower and developed an imaginative sequence about a shower and a seaside swimming pool.

Play also provides for all the other aspects of children's development. They are not likely to develop and learn if their physical growth is retarded; if they are insecure their emotional development is hampered; if they are unable to relate, their social growth is affected. But all these aspects of development are interwoven with each other and with cognitive development. Social development is dependent upon the capacity to relate to oneself, to one's peers and to adults. Emotional development also depends upon a capacity to relate, particularly upon the process of forming a self image. Thus the ability to form a social relationship depends upon emotional stability; young children under emotional stress do not interact easily with other children or adults. Physical development is equally linked with these other aspects of development. Physical skills need to be learnt, and emotional disturbance can make physical control difficult. As is well known, cases have been found of children unable to walk through some hidden malfunction, later shown to have a psychological cause (Rondinesco and Appel 1953). Intellectual growth depends upon all these aspects of development. Children cannot learn effectively unless they maintain their emotional and social equilibrium. If children cannot make relationships they will be handicapped in their learning; the ability to learn must at times depend on the ability to relate to a teacher, whether peer or adult.

13

Play as motivation

Play can be the motivation to learn. All teachers are concerned to motivate children to learn. Punishment, competition and rewards have all been advocated as effective methods of motivation. None of these is necessary to motivate young children to learn through play. Infants who want to set up a pulley to transfer buckets of sand from an outdoor sand pit up a slope, because they are playing at being workmen on a building site, will apply themselves to learn the necessary mechanics of a block and tackle. Play provides reasons children can understand for acquiring the skills and knowledge adults value. When they want to dress up as princesses or pirates, infants see the point in learning to measure accurately in order to cut out and sew. Two seven year old girls carried out some instructions in their mathematics workbooks to measure an awning, and handed in the books. The teacher, finding the answer was obviously wrong, asked the girls if they realized where they had made a mistake. They replied, 'Oh yes, we knew we had forgotten to double the measurements of the side.'

'Why didn't you alter the books then?'

'Oh well, it didn't matter, did it?'

But when they wanted later to make a puppet theatre for their play, it *did* matter that they measured accurately, or the puppet theatre would have collapsed: the motivation was real in the *play* situation.

Teachers know that some children lack interest in books and reading because their experience is limited. They seldom have exciting occurrences to retail verbally or in writing. Often they cannot contribute to discussion; they cannot relate what they read to their everyday life. Schools try hard to compensate; they provide interesting exhibitions, they encourage visitors and take children out of school on visits as often as possible. Play reinforces experiences that schools provide. When at play children are able to absorb and adapt new experiences. They incorporate a picture they have seen, a story heard, or an event experienced in all of the play opportunities provided: in sand, in water, in dressing up, in clay modelling, in painting, in building, in make-believe play. Many will need to play in this way before they are ready to talk, read, write and perhaps think about their experiences. Even older children complain when they are expected to draw or write about a visit immediately after they return to school: they need to play it out or absorb it first.

There can be no doubt that children enjoy play, and there is no doubt that what they enjoy, they will want to go on doing. Enjoyment motivates. When children are motivated, they will persevere, they can overcome difficulties and often concentrate for long periods, and they may put great effort into what they are doing.

Many people argue against play as an educational method, maintaining that it encourages children to believe that all learning is a pleasant occupation; but if play will motivate a child to persevere beyond the point of enjoyment, then why not use the 'play way'?

The teacher's role in play

When the 'play way' of learning was first introduced into infant schools many believed that the teacher was required to do no more than provide the opportunity for children to play. Once children had the opportunity to play, it was said, learning would 'naturally' occur. In the same way, it was maintained that if young children were able to talk freely to each other in school, their use of language would automatically develop. Similarly, some adults expected all children who were surrounded with attractive books to develop the desire to read. Experience, recent research and the observation of teachers have all shown that the provision of opportunity and materials is not sufficient. All children do not learn to read by being 'immersed in books'; dialogue with their peers will not necessarily foster language development: 'Unless there is opportunity and stimulus at school for children to question and try to explain what they are observing, their experiences can remain always a matter of enjoyable play, satisfying immediate interests, instead of leading *in addition* to an increase in intellectual understanding about the world and facility in thinking scientifically, mathematically and logically' (Brearley and Hitchfield 1966). Play can become repetitive, without aim, devoid of cognitive learning.

There is therefore an important corollary to the evidence that cognitive development takes place through play; this development does not occur without a teacher's help and participation. Children left alone to play do not develop imaginatively; after a time much of their play becomes repetitive and lacking in progression.

Smilansky's work in Israel (1968) led her to conclude that children who play on their own reach an imitative stage of play but do not progress further. The same conclusion has been reached by Tough (1976), that in play children's language develops well only when a teacher takes part, talking to them and stimulating them with questions.

Without the help of a teacher setting the environment and providing the suggestions, children reach stalemate and their play becomes intellectually aimless. The bridge referred to earlier between

15

the symbolic and real remains unbuilt, and learning does not take place. A skilled teacher can point the children's enquiry, provide new materials, stimulate discussion or bring out new possibilities in an existing situation: 'Much of the children's play is cultural and needs adult participation so that external facts and their significance can be communicated' (DES 1967).

References

BREARLEY, M. and HITCHFIELD, E. (1966) *A Teacher's Guide to Reading Piaget* Routledge and Kegan Paul

BRUNER, J. S. (1966) *Studies in Cognitive Growth* John Wiley

DES (1967) *Children and their Primary Schools* (Plowden Report) HMSO

FURTH, H. G. and WACHS, H. (1974) *Thinking Goes to School: Piaget's Theory in Practice* Oxford University Press

ISAACS, S. (1930) *Intellectual Growth in Young Children* Routledge and Kegan Paul

ISAACS, S. (1933) *Social Development in Young Children* Routledge and Kegan Paul

PARRY, M. and ARCHER, H. (1975) *Two to Five* Macmillan Education

PIAGET, J. (1951) *Play, Dreams and Imitation in Childhood* Routledge and Kegan Paul

PIAGET, J. (1969) *Science of Education and The Psychology of the Child* Longman

SMILANSKY, S. (1968) *The Effects of Sociodramatic Play on Disadvantaged Preschool Children* John Wiley

TOUGH, J. (1976) *Listening to Children Talking* Ward Lock Educational

Film

RONDINESCO, J. and APPEL, G. (1953) *Maternal Deprivation in Young Children* 16 mm film available from Concord Film Council Limited, Ipswich, Suffolk

Suggestions for further reading can be found in the book list in Appendix 2.

The basis for *structuring* play is observing and taking your cues from the *children's* spontaneous play.

Children learn from each other when they play together.

Moving play outdoors enables children to have the space and make the mess necessary to concentrate on their exploratory play.

The teacher who has shared in the children's play is able to incorporate it into their other activities.

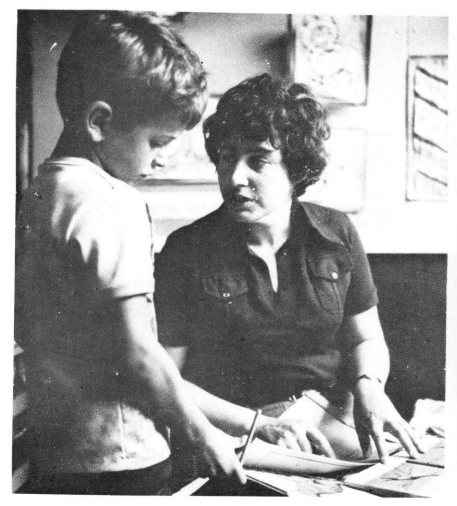

2 Structuring play

We have described play as an all-embracing activity of central significance in the infant school. Its significance is as a vehicle for all aspects of young children's learning, development and motivation. But if play in the infant school is to promote children's learning, it must be structured. This structure must enable them to gain the maximum learning and development latent in play combined with the maximum enjoyment. Without structure play cannot be used as a teaching and learning medium. A teacher's job is to teach, by which we mean to ensure that children learn. Teachers should not provide for play as part of the infant school curriculum without finding time to structure it.

This Project's interpretation of structuring does not mean a rigid set of conditions and rules into which children's play is forced. Nothing is further from our intentions. On the contrary, the Project found that structuring children's play is a successful learning situation only when the teacher builds on the children's spontaneous play and takes her cues from the children.

When structuring play, teachers must leave the children with freedom of choice. If play is structured in such a way that children are given no opportunity to select their own materials, space, time and playmates, or to develop their own ideas, teachers defeat their object: the children stop playing. To structure play we must look at it through *adults'* eyes to see all the learning that is possible; we must look at it through *children's* eyes to structure it in such a way that it is accepted by the children.

The Project defined structuring as:

1 Provision: providing space; providing adequate time for play; providing materials to start play, maintain it and develop its potential; removing materials when they are ignored or have served their purpose; making rules to safeguard the children, protect equipment and enable the play to occur in school.

2   The acceptance of an active role by the teacher who joins in the children's play, to further each learning situation and promote physical, social and emotional development. Three kinds of teacher involvement were identified in the Project: participation, initiation and intervention.

Structuring is based on observation

At every stage in the structuring of play the importance of taking cues from the children is emphasized. In order to do this teachers must *observe*. Unless they observe children's needs, backgrounds, personalities and stages of development, they cannot provide suitable space, time, materials or rules. Observation is not only the basis of provision but also the bridge linking it with adult involvement. Successful teacher involvement is entirely dependent on observation; e.g. only by observing will a teacher know how to help children solve a problem, be able to work out whether they will understand the solution, and know whether their interest is sufficient to warrant further experiment. In other words, she will have different objectives for different children at different times. She will not expect children to pursue problems that require thinking of a kind that they are not able to cope with. Nor will she want them to continue activities long after they have explored all the possibilities.

Mistakes can be made if an adult has not observed; for example, a teacher recording for the Project described a six year old girl playing with shells in the sand tray. The girl had been inventing a story with the shells. As an experienced welfare assistant passed by she noticed the child's obvious absorption and wanted to show interest. Seeing the girl moving her finger delicately around the shells, she said:

> Those shells are very pretty, aren't they? Doesn't the sand feel soft and smooth on your fingers – is it tickling? You have made a lovely pattern. Have you finished it or are you going to put more shells or something else in it?

She made three attempts to promote discussion and join in the play but failed. The teacher observing the play knew why: the shells were representing people and trees, and the finger was a cat taking a walk! Unless a teacher has observed carefully she will not know what stage in his play each individual child has reached.

Repetition in play

Repetition is a basic feature in children's play. Children need to repeat their play so that an experience can be absorbed, a role understood, and to reinforce what has been learned. They need time to consolidate their mastery, develop confidence and expand their self image. Unless a teacher has observed carefully, she will not know whether the children need to repeat their play, or whether it has reached stalemate: repetitive play reaches stalemate when it has become purposeless and the children are neither learning nor developing. The teacher can only tell from observation what help the children need to develop their play: whether they need a new idea or new materials because they have repeated their play sufficiently and cannot extend it by themselves; or whether they need help because their insecurity causes them to repeat the same play continually. Teachers know some children fear failure and dare not proceed of their own accord to a new activity. Even when they are at play, they avoid the novel situation. Success and praise only make them repeat the activity because it gives them security.

A teacher introduces new elements into this play to enable children to move from such repetition which has become purposeless. These new elements which constitute structuring play are:

1 provision
2 teacher involvement.

Within the overall framework of the school's building and philosophy individual teachers formulate their own classroom structure.

Provision

Space
When teachers allocate certain areas within the classroom or school to specific forms of play, they are imposing a form of structure on that play. A group of children confining their domestic play to the space within a 'Wendy house' frame will not develop their imaginative ideas in the same way as children with space to have two houses. A long narrow corridor space may dictate the form of layout of a roadway or aerodrome. When a large floor space in the school hall is provided for brick building and other constructions, the play is being structured; it enables the children to experiment and be imaginative in a different way from construction play that takes place on a small carpet.

Time
The amount of time children are given to play imposes another form

of structure. It is difficult to estimate exactly how long each child needs to play with the same materials or ideas. One child or one group of children will play with certain materials on one occasion for several hours: the same child or group will play with the same materials on another occasion for a few minutes only. This is not because they have exhausted the possibilities of the materials, for subsequently they may spend several days playing with the same materials. The factors that determine the length of time children devote to play are numerous – the distraction of novelty in the surrounding environment, to mention but one. Despite this problem of knowing how much time children need to develop play situations to the full, it would seem logical to argue that children who are given unlimited time for play are more likely to be able to devise imaginative situations, to follow through their discoveries and work out their problems than children whose play has often been cut short at the most interesting point. If children know from experience that play in school must be completed within a short time, or if left unfinished cannot be carried over to another time or day, then they 'adapt' their play to suit this time allocation.

Materials

Children's play in school is dependent to a certain extent on the materials and equipment available; for example, exploratory play is more advanced if both dry and wet sand are provided, if equipment for sieving as well as floating and sinking is at hand. Large constructions leading to imaginative play cannot be made with small building materials. Thus teachers structure play by providing or withholding materials and equipment in accordance with the children's interests and the potential learning revealed. For instance, if they know that the children are acquiring concepts of shape, they provide matching sets of cups, saucers and plates in different shapes for domestic play, a variety of shaped bricks and boxes for construction play, and a choice of different shapes for collage and for make-believe play.

The storage and availability of materials are themselves a form of structuring. Bright, attractive and easily available materials are as essential to stimulate play as they are for other school activities.

Rules

Teachers make rules about play for many reasons: sometimes the reasons are within their control and sometimes they are not. If the teacher limits the number of children playing at domestic play to a maximum of four, or if children are restricted in shop play to the purchase of two articles, these rules are voluntary on her part. If, on the other hand, she is forced to limit the number because of lack of classroom space, the structure is not of her making. When all the class activities must be contained in one room, rules must be made that affect movement and noise. These change the nature of the play; the children accept the limitation and adapt their play accordingly.

Teachers also make rules about the use of materials and equipment. Some do not permit materials to be combined, which may prevent make-believe play from occurring, discoveries from being made, problems from being solved; it may direct the way play develops; it is definitely another form of structure.

Sometimes rules have to be made because of the children's home background and previous experience. Some children do not know how to organize their play if they are given unrestricted choice of materials. Others do not know how to care for materials or use them in a socially acceptable manner. Teachers make rules to help these children adapt to the play situation in school. They review them regularly, recognizing that the need for rules that structure play may change.

Teacher involvement

Participation

Participation is the term used to describe the teacher's role when joining in children's play, i.e. sharing it in such a way that the children recognize the adult as a participator, not an interrogator or an interested outsider or a congratulating encourager. We have identified a role when teachers participate and we believe this role is important if they wish to understand what is happening in the play, and to show children that teachers value and enjoy playing.

Many teachers find the role of participator the most difficult to undertake in children's play. Some maintain that children do not want them to join in their play. They argue that as soon as an adult participates, the design of the play is changed; the children are no longer able to be in charge; they either look to the adult for guidance or withdraw. The teachers in the Project found that those who enjoy play are able to share in it without directing or dominating. These are the teachers whom children welcome and invite into their play; they are able to join in while still maintaining their identity as adults.

The teacher can also play alongside the children, making her own model or sand castle but not actually joining in their play. This kind of teacher involvement gives the children the opportunity to ignore the teacher and continue in their own play if they wish, to withdraw altogether, to carry on their own play while absorbing how the teacher is playing, to imitate her, to adapt her play and incorporate it into their own, to share in the teacher's play or invite her to share in theirs. It establishes a rapport through a shared and enjoyable experience, and it shows children that teachers value play and give time to it themselves.

'The teacher can play alongside the children making her own model but not actually joining in their play.'

A teacher's attitude to play is related to the importance she attaches to play as a learning process. Similarly, children's attitude to play in school is related to the teacher's. They are not so likely to concentrate, persevere and devote time to play if they know that the teacher is not interested, or does not find time to participate. It becomes evident to them that play is not a highly valued activity in school. It is generally accepted that a teacher's class will reflect her interests and enthusiasm. If she finds the children's play exciting, stimulating and worthwhile, so will they. Teachers who join in children's play find the children are in no doubt that it is a valued activity. These teachers are able to relate what happens in the play to other school activities and to incorporate such activities naturally into the play. When they are sharing the play they find it easy to develop ideas, introduce skills, identify problems, advise about solutions and foster language. Children are less likely to resent suggestions which come from an adult whom they have accepted into their play. Sharing children's play means establishing a relationship with them of accepting and being accepted. Once established in play, this relationship can be carried over into all the teaching and learning situations.

Initiation

Initiation may be a form of participation; it will often involve provision, and always result from observation. We understand initiation to be an attempt on the teacher's part to show the children a new skill, or to give them new information that will enable them to develop an existing play situation or devise a fresh one. It may take the form of a suggestion that extends the play in a way the children had not planned themselves, the provision of knowledge or materials, or sources of knowledge and materials, that the children were not aware could further their play. It may be discussion and questioning that lead the children to devise new play situations or develop existing ones. But whatever form it takes, the teacher's intention is that her initiation will result in new developments in the play, which the children are able to continue on their own.

We know that children may reject attempts to initiate; for example, they will not incorporate suggestions into subsequent play. We give reasons why this may happen which may help teachers not to be discouraged and to understand the cause:

1   We may have misinterpreted the children's understanding of their play situation.
2   We may have misjudged their ability, and initiated play that is too difficult for them to pursue without adult help.
3   New interests may occur that lead the play in directions we could not have foreseen.
4   Children may use our suggestions in a completely different way from that we intended.
5   The new ideas may not be taken up immediately. It may be much later that we recognize them being incorporated into the play.
6   Our suggestions may be woven into another area of play.
7   We may have chosen the wrong time and need to try again at a more opportune time. The children may be too absorbed in another aspect of the play to attend to the one we are highlighting.

Intervention

Initiation and intervention are allied: often intervention leads to initiation, but there are occasions when a teacher intervenes without intending to initiate new play situations. Only observation and knowledge of the children tell the teacher when to intervene or *not* to intervene. She intervenes:

1   when the children have a problem they cannot solve
2   when she can lead them to reach a logical conclusion
3   when one or more children are disrupting the play
4   when the children are at risk because equipment or materials are being abused
5   when the play is interfering with the activities of other children in the classroom
6   when the play has reached stalemate.

The teacher does *not* intervene:

1   until she has given the children time to work out the solution to their problem or resolve their disagreements
2   unless she knows that they are capable of comprehending the logical conclusion
3   when the repetitive play is serving a purpose.

PART 2

Using play in the classroom

Introduction

Having discussed the premises on which the Project was based, we now come to the main objective of the book: to show teachers how play can be structured in their classrooms to make it a learning process for the children. We do this by describing and analysing children's play in the classroom. All the play described has come from the Project teachers' recordings. The examples of play are typical of the thousands that we received, although no two were identical as each teacher took her cues from her own children.

For many teachers, play is the basis of the curriculum; they provide for play throughout the day and use it as the central agent and motivating force for all the child's learning. Other teachers provide for play at different times during the day, using it for some learning activities but not for all. This book will be useful for both types of organization, since all teachers need to examine carefully the play that takes place in their rooms, whether they provide for play all day and every day or only at specified times. They must know why they are providing this play and what they intend the children to gain from it. Then they are able to work out what kind of organization will best achieve these objectives in their situation: how much time is needed, what kinds of materials are required, how much space can be allocated, whether any rules should be made, what kind of involvement a teacher must have.

All will have to be decided within the total context of the infant curriculum, particularly when deciding how much time a teacher can spare to be involved in play. She has many other tasks in the classroom. Children need to be taught 'skills' such as those necessary for reading or mathematics. They do not just 'pick up' these skills by chance in their play and time will need to be set aside by the teacher to teach children, for example how to spell. Precisely when she does this, and how she organizes it, depends on her own particular situation and philosophy.

There is no suggestion in our descriptions of play that the teacher is involved only in play; many other activities are equally important and make equal demands. In fact the teacher needs to make sure she does not overstructure. She should not make the mistake of thinking that she must be involved in all the children's play. They need to play on their own, to try out and sometimes discard the suggestions made by an adult. Once a teacher has taken part in the play, children often show that they are able to transfer the ideas to another situation and to develop them in a way unforeseen by the teacher. However, we do not believe there is any danger of overinterference by the teacher engaged with the full range of activities undertaken by a large group of infants. Nevertheless this is something she will have to consider if she is fortunate enough to have the assistance of many parents in school. Children can be overwhelmed by too many suggestions and ideas and by 'too much joining in, too much encouragement, too much taking the lead, too frequent switching of children's attention – what I like to call the "grandparent syndrome"' (Tinbergen 1975).

Reference
TINBERGEN, N. (1975) The importance of being playful *Times Educational Supplement* 10 January

3 How the Project studied play

Categories

To enable teachers in the classroom to look at play, the Project divided it into five categories. The categories were chosen to cover children's most common play activities. When young children play, they build, play house, devise make/believe situations, use a variety of natural materials, run, leap and climb. We excluded from our work all kinds of manufactured games (made by teacher or supplier) often so structured that they can be used in one way only.

Use of the term Make/Believe

Make/Believe with a stroke (/) is a term we have devised to describe the category of play that covers children's making *and* make-believing. In the first stage of the Project there were two categories of play that covered children's creative activities and dressing up. As a result of the teachers' observations and recordings these two were combined and the special Make/Believe category devised. This is the descriptive term that teachers in the second stage of the Project found acceptable. We also use make-believe with a hyphen (-) in the conventional sense to describe children's pretend play.

Although all the different kinds of play overlap, teachers have found that by dividing play and focusing on each category in turn, they could ensure that the provision was adequate, stimuli were there, and that they could identify how and when they should become involved in the play (by participating, initiating and intervening).

Domestic: Play in the Wendy house, or home corner, mothers and fathers, doll play, and all the play that arises out of this, e.g. washing, cleaning, cooking, shopping, hospitals.

Construction: Play with small and large bricks, large and

	small constructional toys, junk constructional materials.
Make/Believe:	Play with paint, crayons, scrap, collage and dressing-up materials that involves the children in making and pretending.
Natural Materials:	Play with wet and dry sand, water, clay, wood and other natural materials, for example shells, stones, conkers.
Outdoors:	The four categories of play listed above, but taking place outside, and play stimulated by the outside environment and equipment.

These categories frequently overlap: constructions are made in the sand, make/believe also occurs in domestic play. Similarly the same kind of learning may occur in them all, for example in problem solving.

Stimuli

The stimuli for all the play also overlap. Not all the stimuli will be present in all the play but teachers' reports show the following as the main ones:

1 experiences based on the home
2 experiences shared by several children, often in school, e.g. visitors, police, fire-service, dentist
3 stories and poems
4 television or films
5 expeditions
6 local environment.

Play descriptions

The objectives of the play descriptions are:

1 to show teachers the kind of play that can be developed with an average class, using the play materials that are available in most infant schools
2 to give examples of the motivation, learning and development that can arise from play
3 to show the different kinds of adult involvement that can occur in play and how these are necessary to develop the play
4 to provide examples of play that teachers can adapt to their own use.

The descriptions are not meant to be 'models' or copied as 'play lessons'. Every school, every classroom, every child and every teacher is different and the ideas must be adapted to every situation. It should also be remembered that all children need to play on their own in order to develop their own ideas and personalities.

In the descriptions, readers will find some repetition; since this is a reference and resource book the basic ideas are illustrated in many places. Nevertheless each category of play has a different emphasis in content and style. The descriptions of the categories of play are developed so that teachers can build up their own skills in observing and analysing. The situations become more complicated as the book progresses. We stress that if examples of children's language or adult involvement do not appear in every description of play, it is not because thay were not present but because when teachers are new to observing and analysing play it is better to concentrate on one aspect at a time. It is important that the categories are studied in the order in which they are written.

Age range

The descriptions of play cover the age range from the 'rising-five' to the seven year old. We include in the descriptions ideas that are suited to both younger and older children, knowing that teachers will select accordingly. Although the Project looked at play in the first school and had examples from the eight to nine age range, there were too few to reproduce any examples as typical for this age range.

Materials

The materials most commonly used in schools are listed in each kind of play. These are not completely comprehensive nor are they prescriptive lists. They indicate the type of materials which give rise to the play we mention and teachers need to use their own initiative to exploit local resources, e.g. in one Project school, a father owned a television shop and gave the school an unending supply of extra-large cardboard boxes.

Motivation, learning and development

Examples of motivation, learning and development are given after each description of play. We describe children's physical, social, emotional and cognitive development as learning and development, recognizing that some educationists prefer to use the term learning to cover all aspects of children's development, and others, for example Furth (1970), maintain that all children's learning is part of their development and that therefore one should refer to the development of children. Once again the lists given after each play description are not fully comprehensive or prescriptive. They indicate the kind of learning and development that can arise in play; for example, emotional and social development, mathematical and scientific concepts, language, new vocabulary needed by the children to extend the play, physical and manipulative skills. (Wherever we discuss language the terms used are those found in *Listening to Children Talking* by Joan Tough, 1976.) As we said in the preface teachers need to refer to specialists' publications in these fields to ensure that they know exactly what steps a child must go through in learning to read, for example. We list in Appendix 2 some books that we have found useful for this.

It must however be remembered that the kinds of learning and development that occur will depend on the background and experience of the children and on how the play is structured.

Adults in the play

Readers will note that the adults who appear in the various play situations are of all the kinds that can be met in the infant school, including non-teaching staff and parents. There is no special significance in the appearance of a welfare assistant: it usually depended on where the play description came from; for example, many of our areas used nursery nurses in their reception classes.

The adult involvement is analysed in the play descriptions to show the learning and development that can occur when adults take part in the play. Although children constantly make discoveries in their play the teacher must look for them and be ready with her ideas and language to develop them through the play. The examples given show how the teacher structures the play to further this development.

The development and sequence of the play categories

1 Domestic Play

We consider domestic play first because the foundation of structuring is taking cues from the children. All domestic play is based on children's home experience, which provides cues teachers can recognize. This probably explains why teachers have found this the easiest kind of play to start observing and analysing. Although teachers thought they were familiar with this play, when they observed it more closely they discovered that very often it was much more complex than they had realized.

Domestic Play describes the kinds of activities that take place under our definition of this category of play. Since there is so much of this category and teachers are most familiar with it, we have kept the descriptions short and omitted children's language.

These descriptions are analysed for motivation, learning and development and the materials are listed. We have also omitted teacher involvement in this section as we wanted the reader initially to concentrate on the motivation, learning and development and consider provision.

Two of the play descriptions are left for teachers to analyse. Our own analysis for comparison can be found in Appendix 1.

2 Construction Play

Construction Play follows because we have based our descriptions of this play on the stimuli that inspire it. After observing the cues children give in domestic play for adults to develop, teachers realize that there are many other kinds of stimuli that give rise to children's play. These were especially obvious in the recordings of construction play. These stimuli do of course apply to all play but it is intended that teachers should look at them in detail at this stage.

The descriptions of construction play describe actual situations in the classroom. They are fairly brief descriptions so that readers are not overwhelmed with a mass of detail when analysing for themselves. In Construction Play we ask the question 'How did the teacher structure this play?' and suggest answers.

One example is left for teachers to analyse for themselves.

3 Make/Believe Play

We now describe the play in much more detail and give examples of the children's language. The analysis of the motivation, learning and development in the play continues but the adult's involvement is elaborated and more questions are asked and answered than previously.

Once again one situation is left for teachers to analyse.

4 Play with Natural Materials

In this chapter we take a step forward and look at the abstract concepts apparently aroused in the children by the materials themselves. We found that teachers' recordings of play with natural materials divided themselves into three types: sensory, imaginative and exploratory, and we have therefore described the play under these headings. It is of course possible to identify these headings in the other categories and teachers could try this for themselves.

This chapter is much longer than the others because we have described the play with four different kinds of materials.

By now teachers will be practised in analysing the play descriptions. Therefore we have only analysed play in this section where it has special significance. Questions are given for teachers to answer.

5   *Play Outdoors*

Play Outdoors includes the four categories of play described earlier, showing how new dimensions can be given to them outside and what kind of play arises from the outdoor environment and equipment.

It considers at length the problems in providing for play outdoors. It was these problems that were the teachers' main concern in this category of play.

Once again questions are included.

Using the chapters on play

Since this is a reference and resource book teachers need to do more than read it to gain the full benefit of the ideas and suggestions made. As well as the play descriptions to analyse and the points for discussion, each of the following chapters in Part 2 has practical suggestions for classroom activities. These are marked with this symbol

All the categories of play have specific suggestions for the teacher to try out. The following activities however apply to *each* category of play.

1   Before trying out any of the activities suggested the teacher should look at the children to see:
   (a) if they are playing
   (b) how they are playing
   (c) what materials they are using
   (d) what is happening as a result.
2   While the teacher is trying out the specific activities she needs to:
   (a) examine the provision: space, time, materials and rules, and decide if the structure needs revising
   (b) examine the amount of adult involvement, and decide whether all the opportunities for participation, initiation and intervention have been used.

Teachers should not feel overwhelmed by the numbers of ideas and activities suggested and think 'My children can't possibly do this'. Six hundred Project teachers have proved it is possible to structure play in the way we have described. Despite initial misgivings, when they became involved in the play and provided space, time and new materials, they found that all the developments we describe are possible. These teachers came from every type of school and situation and were successful only because they adapted the suggestions made to their own classroom and took their cues from their own children.

We must stress that the activities suggested cannot be hurried. It takes time to try out new ideas, to alter classroom procedures. We urge any teacher who tries to work as we suggest to allow the children and herself time to adapt and develop the play. It is important not to expect immediate 'results'; for example, if the teacher takes the children out to look at a building site this may not influence the construction play at the time but many weeks later she may observe in domestic play 'father' using a cardboard tube as a pneumatic drill when he goes to work.

We also urge teachers where possible to work and discuss with colleagues: much can be gained by exchanging ideas and suggesting solutions to each other's problems.

All the examples of play in the following pages were recorded by teachers working with the Project. They all describe quality play, i.e. play that has the following qualities:

1 It enables the children to learn and develop.
2 It is sustained over a period of time.
3 It is carried through to a conclusion that the children find satisfying; that gives rise to perseverance and concentration.
4 It is absorbing for the individual children concerned.
5 It is enjoyed and shared by a group of children, albeit to differing degrees.

We have had so many examples similar to these from the Project teachers that we have no doubt that any teacher reading this book will find she can adapt the descriptions to her own use.

References
FURTH, H. G. (1970) *Piaget for Teachers* Prentice-Hall
TOUGH, J. (1976) *Listening to Children Talking* Ward Lock Educational

4 Domestic Play

Introduction

We have explained earlier that we describe Domestic Play first because it stems from experiences that are familiar to all children and teachers.

We have left the analysis of the last two play descriptions to teachers. Our analysis of the motivation, learning and development can be found in Appendix 1.

The eight kinds of domestic play which we have selected were recorded by the teachers working with the Project. This traditional home play may occur with or without the provision of domestic play materials whenever groups of young children are together or even when they are at solitary play. The majority of teachers in the Project favoured a home corner. Therefore we purposely suggest play that could arise from this.

Mothers and fathers

When children play 'at house' they are invariably playing some form of 'mothers and fathers and children'. The records kept by teachers reveal that the activities revolve around eating meals, preparing meals, father going to work and coming home for meals, washing up, cleaning the house, getting dressed, going shopping, telephoning, being ill and doll play. Much of this play takes place very rapidly and the adult has to be quick to observe that a meal has been prepared, served, eaten and cleared away in a matter of minutes or even seconds. A sick child can have been put to bed, diagnosed, treated, and returned to health before the adult realizes what is occurring.

Children can be helped to extend all of this play by the provision of extra equipment (occasionally 'real materials'), by the questions and discussion of an adult and by the participation of a sympathetic teacher.

Sometimes the play can be sustained and extended without real materials, e.g. cooking, but at other times the real experience makes imaginary play more realistic and prolonged. There is obvious satisfaction for the children in the rapid play described, but our observations have shown that if this continues the children grow tired of it and eventually leave the 'home corner' or use it for other purposes.

There are some children who are not at home long enough with their parents to observe the cleaning, cooking and other activities mentioned and they will need to play with an adult and other children before they become aware of why domestic play materials are provided in school. Children from different cultural backgrounds may need to play house in a different way and will introduce new ideas into the domestic play.

At one time only a small corner of the classroom was set apart for domestic play, but teachers are becoming increasingly aware of the need to provide adequate space for all the extensions that can come out of domestic play. Children sometimes need more than one room; a sitting or dining room and a bedroom. They may need more than one house to accommodate the number of children involved or allow for two families. The shop, the clinic, or the doctor's surgery may need to be near the house. For this reason the restricting Wendy house is often discarded and domestic play occurs in the corridor or adapted cloakroom space or in a carpeted quiet room.

Examples of motivation, learning and development that may occur in this play

1 Emotional development from the opportunity to enact disturbing experiences; to shout at mother, father, husband, child, to blame another for an accident or mistake and to dramatize experiences.

2 Social development from being 'boss' or baby, sharing experiences with peers and adults, cooperating in play, experiencing family relationships.

3 Language. Children use language in this play for reasoning: 'You've got to get up now 'cos she's sick and she must be in bed when the doctor comes.'

They report what is happening, drawing on previous experience: 'I must get a basket. My mummy never goes shopping without her basket.'

They use language in their imaginative play: 'Doctor you'll have to come, she's got a temperature. I can't bring her to the surgery. She feels ever so hot.'

They use language to direct other children: 'You haven't put enough cups and saucers. There's four of us. Put the plates there. Now we want knives and forks.'

They maintain their position and authority in the play: 'Give me that newspaper. You can't have it, you're the baby. I'm Dad, I read the newspaper. Give it me.'

They predict the course of events: 'Hurry up with that cooking. When your dad comes in he'll want his dinner ready.'

They project into the behaviour of others, imagining their reactions: 'I'm keeping my eyes shut because I'm poorly in bed and the light hurts my eyes.'

4 New vocabulary needed: husband, nephew, niece, wardrobe,

bedside cabinet, duvet, eiderdown, housekeeping allowance, salary, plumber, telephone engineer.

5 Development of mathematical concepts, one to one correspondence.
6 Development of scientific concepts, e.g. dissolving, melting, heating up.
7 Manipulative skill in using equipment.
8 Physical skill in using larger materials.
9 Experience of sound.
10 Motivation to observe household events and recall the sequence in order to imitate.
11 Motivation to read and write, e.g. shopping lists, recipes, washing instructions.

Materials
1 House furniture, or equipment such as boxes and tubs which can be adapted for the purpose, tables, chairs, child-sized bed, sleeping bag, mattress or rug, cupboard, stove.
2 Dressing-up clothes.
3 Equipment for a meal: matching cups and saucers, plates, jug, teapot, coffee pot, cutlery – not miniature, real but the size that can be handled by children, condiments, sauce bottles.
4 Equipment for cooking, cleaning, doll play, shop play, 'sick' play.

Dolls
Children are often observed by their teacher playing with dolls in the home corner. They talk to each other about the dolls and their play. Sometimes they dress the dolls preparatory to taking them out for a walk. They may discuss the dolls' clothes as they try them on but show no method in the way they make their final choice, folding and wrapping large garments to make them fit a doll. After the dolls are dressed they are put in a pram or a push chair and taken for a walk in the room or along the corridor.

Often the children dress up and play in clothes from the dressing-up box that fit their ideas of mothers and fathers, the girls especially having a handbag or shopping basket when they are taking baby out.

Suggestions for developing this play
1 Dolls' clothes could be provided in sets matched for size, colour and pattern.
2 Dolls' bed clothes, pram covers and equipment could be

provided matched in similar fashion.

3 An adult could join in the conversation and promote discussion about the selection of clothes for babies and the way in which mothers dress their babies.

4 A mother might be invited into school with her baby to bath and dress, and to discuss these operations with a group of children.

5 The children could be encouraged to describe the dolls and dolls' clothes they have at home, e.g. Cindy dolls, Action Men.

6 The children could be encouraged to walk their prams indoors, in the playground or around the playing field if space is restricted.

7 A collection of dolls' clothes and sets of dolls dressed in different ways could be made.

8 An expedition to a toy or doll museum could be arranged.

9 Reference could be made to pictures of different kinds of dolls.

10 Magazines or catalogues could be consulted in discussions about children's clothes and fashions.

11 A visit to the shops could be arranged to look at baby clothes, toys, toilet requisites.

12 Dolls' clothes and bed and pram covers could be made by older infants, possibly including fabric printing or tie-dyeing. If sewing is too difficult they can be stapled.

13 Rag or newspaper dolls could be made and dressed.

14 Books about babies' clothes could be compiled.

15 Baby foods and toilet requisites could be collected to sell in the shop.

16 Discussion on babies' toys could be held.

17 Discussion of hygiene and safety first in care of babies could take place.

18 Babies and dolls could be weighed and measured.

19 Stories about dolls and babies could be read and told.

20 Stories about dolls and dolls' families and dolls' houses could be written or taped.

21 Doll play could be combined with shop play or other domestic play.

Examples of motivation, learning and development that may occur in this play

1 Emotional development in understanding mother's time and attention given to babies.

2 Cooperation in sharing equipment.

3 Social experience of sharing baby care with adults.

4 Language. Children use language in doll play for reasoning;

40

'I'm putting this coat on her 'cos it's yellow and it matches this hat. It's got the same yellow dots.'

They report what is happening as they play, recalling their observations from first-hand experience: 'I'm patting her gently with the towel. I have to dry her all over 'cos her skin will chap.'

They use language in the imaginary situation: 'Don't cry, I'm not hurting you but I must get this nose clean. It will soon be over.'

They use speech to direct other children: 'You can empty the water now. I've finished bathing the baby. Mind you don't spill it.'

Language helps them to maintain their position: 'I wheel the pram. I'm the mother. You can hold the baby when we get back but I've got to wheel her out.'

They predict in speech what will happen next: 'If you hold her like that she'll cry.'

They project into the feelings of others: 'Ooh there's a good boy. Have you got a smile for your mummy?'

5 New vocabulary needed: trolley, cradle, bootees, dungarees, elasticated, snug, miniature, lukewarm, thermometer, absorbent, perambulator.
6 Mathematical experience of shopping.
7 Practice in making sets, e.g. night clothes, indoor and outdoor clothes.
8 Practice in matching size, shape, colour, pattern.
9 Practical experience of measurement and weight.
10 Scientific experience in washing clothes and regulating the temperature of the water.
11 Manipulative skill in dressing and undressing dolls.
12 Physical skill in manoeuvring prams.
13 Motivation to observe carefully and recall experience.
14 Motivation to remember sequence of events.
15 Motivation to consult books, magazines, catalogues.
16 Motivation to read, draw, write, record on tape.
17 Motivation to concentrate and complete a task.

Materials
1 Dolls, graded in size.
2 Dolls' beds, cots or cradles, graded in size.
3 Dolls' pram and push chair.
4 Dolls' clothes, graded in size and matched in sets by colour or pattern and with varied methods of fastening.

5 Dolls' bed and pram covers in different sizes and colours.
6 Miniature families of dolls or Lego or similar materials for making them.
7 Rooms or boxes that can be used as houses for miniature doll play.
8 Miniature furniture, wooden or plastic shapes, or Lego for miniature doll play, scrap materials for making dolls' furniture and clothes.
9 Equipment for bathing a baby, plastic bath, or classroom sink, towels, talcum powder, cotton-wool buds.
10 Comb, brush.
11 Magazines and catalogues.
12 Books about babies and dolls.
13 Baby scales.
14 Equipment for measuring.

Shopping

What kind of shop?
The most commonly found shop in infant schools is the traditional grocer's shop stocked with used packets and empty tins. In schools that provide real groceries the children gain more satisfaction in their play and are having the experience of handling true weights. Similarly the provision of real money ensures correct counting and accounting at the end of the play session. It also gives purpose to the bank which can stand alongside the shop where the cashier can draw the money for the shop and bank his takings as part of the play. Obviously shop play varies according to the age, ability and experience of the children. Very young children are content to offer money in exchange for goods and always expect 'change' as well. Older children are able to keep accounts, check expenditure and change, deal in larger amounts and weigh accurately.

Teachers structure shop play in different ways; for example, by specifying that only three articles may be purchased by one customer in each session; by limiting and varying the amount of money each child has to spend.

Many children may not be familiar with the grocer's shop in their real-life experience and few local grocers provide the experience of weighing that is normally included in school. Some children are not familiar with the greengrocer's and do not see goods weighed; vegetables and fruit are frequently bought prepacked in the supermarket. It may be difficult to devise shop situations that involve weighing that are within the children's experience.

Setting up shop

Before setting up shop in school the teacher needs to know what kind of shops the children are familiar with. She also needs to take small groups of children out shopping so that they all have a common experience to discuss.

There are many reasons for going to buy goods that the children use in school: for example, ingredients for cooking; nails, screws and wood for woodwork; cleaning materials for domestic play. After such expeditions and discussions with the children about the kind of shop they would like to have in school, the teacher can work out how she can ensure that all the possibilities of shopping are realized.

A few shelves, a bench or a table and cash register for the check-out with some baskets for the customers will serve as a supermarket

If the children decide to have a supermarket or serve-yourself grocery and greengrocery, much time will be spent preparing the goods and deciding how they should be displayed. A few shelves, a bench or table and a cash register for the check-out, with some baskets for the customers, will serve as a supermarket. All goods will need to be priced and weighed so that the weight can be clearly marked. Posters and price lists will need to be prepared for display. If it is decided not to have a supermarket or grocery, schools have found a chemist's or ironmonger's are within the children's experience; they give a change from the normal classroom shop and fit into the needs of domestic play. In some areas a weekly market is held and the children want to set up stalls. If the classroom is not large enough, corridors or the playground provide suitable space. The children enjoy decorating the awnings, and making the super-structure gives purpose to measuring and woodwork. A fish and chip shop is within the experience of the majority of infant school children and one of our schools has recorded play in the 'Chippie'. Similarly, boys and girls are familiar with the hairdresser's, and it is easy to improvise hairdryers, provide rollers, hairnets, ear shields, metal hand mirrors, and overalls.

Price lists, notices, labels and advertisements are needed for all these shops, and for the hairdresser's a knowledge of time for an appointments book. If good cooking facilities are available the children can bake the biscuits for sale at breaktime or the biscuits can be sold in a café during the course of the morning. The class bank issues tokens that are 'spent' on the milk, and the cashier checks at the end of the morning to record the numbers of tokens taken and cartons of milk drunk. A café or Wimpy Bar is a very popular adjunct to house play and gives many opportunities for combining cooking, milk time, family play and shopping.

Older children are able to play in a post office. Preparation for this merits several visits, ideally to a main post office. Parcels can be wrapped and weighed and the cost worked out. Stamps of different denominations can be painted, gummed and perforated. Postal orders, dog and television licences can be prepared and greetings telegram forms designed. Children in the class can each be given a telephone number, and a telephone directory can be made. A telephone kiosk can be contrived from a large cardboard container and this will give reality to telephone conversations in the house play. A street directory can be written and kept in the post office for reference purposes to help the children know their area. The post box and postman can be incorporated in post office and domestic play, and the children can be encouraged to write, post and deliver letters, birthday cards and party invitations.

A draper's shop provides many opportunities for making goods of different sizes that are priced accordingly. Old dresses can be cut up so that they can be sold as lengths of material. This will give the opportunity to measure and work out prices. Lengths of cotton (old sheets, tablecloths) can be printed and patterned and made into lace collars and cuffs and fancy trimmings. If material is unavailable, doilies will serve. Buttons can be collected and either sold singly at different prices or made up on cards in sets. Belts can be made and sold according to length; buckles can be collected and sold by size or intricacy of pattern. Cotton reels look new when covered with coloured paper and balls of knitting wool are usually provided by the children and sold by size or ply.

Most children have experience of a sweet shop and it is possible to make a wide variety of sweets that will give many opportunities for counting and weighing. Flour and salt paste makes a variety of sweets. These can be painted and decorated and placed as small chocolates in chocolate boxes; wrapped firmly in various coloured crepe paper to represent different fruit sweets and sold so many for one, two or five pence; or made into barley sugar sticks, sugar mice and pigs. Small blocks of wood are wrapped in silver paper and placed inside chocolate or Mars Bar or Milky Way wrappers. Plasticine, if it can be spared, can be rolled into liquorice twists and pipes.

Sometimes a stationer's or newsagent's is combined with a sweet shop, or if the children are familiar with the village post office/grocery shop they will want to make an all-purpose store. It may be that there is a neighbouring card shop and that the children will make a variety of greetings cards and picture and story books. They can make mixed collections of stories, or books on definite themes: annuals, fairy story books, cowboy story books, animal story books, poetry books, information books – horses, aeroplanes, space. These books can also be of interesting shapes: long, fat, concertina, house, train shaped.

Children may be interested in making paper flowers to sell in a florist's shop or flower stall. A chemist shop often results from hospital, clinic or surgery play. In one school a successful jewellery shop was popular with boys and girls – the necklaces, pendants, bracelets and brooches were all made by the children. The shops selling goods made by the children may not look as attractive to adults as those selling manufactured goods but they are satisfying to the children and encourage them to write, illustrate and create. Obviously it is not suggested that all of these shops would be in a classroom at the same time. A variety has been described to encourage teachers and children to change when they have grown tired of one type, or the occasion arises through other domestic play.

Examples of motivation, learning and development that may occur in this play

1   Social need to interact with others.
2   Language. In shopping play children use language for reasoning: 'That's dearer because it's a bigger packet.'
    They recall their real-life shopping experiences to report on their play: 'Tomatoes will be on the greengrocery counters.'
    They talk as they imagine: 'I'll buy some sweets for my little girl. She can have them when she comes home from school.'
    They use language to direct the play: 'You have to put the baskets down there. You can't take that one with you out of the shop.'
    They maintain their authority in the play: 'Don't you take his money. I'm the cashier. I'm sitting by the cash register.'
    They predict the actions of others: 'If you put those tins there everyone will knock them down.'
    They project into the feelings of others: 'You take this box of biscuits for your mummy. It isn't what she told you to buy but I'm sure she won't mind. These are just as nice.'
3   New vocabulary needed: drapery, pharmacy, florist, receipt, cosmetics, withdrawal form, registered post, anniversary, customer, check-out assistant.
4   Mathematics: money, weight, measuring, counting.
5   Motivation to observe accurately in shops.
6   Motivation to read and write.
7   Motivation to consult books.
8   Motivation to draw and paint posters and shop fronts.
9   Motivation to construct shop fronts.
10 Motivation to make goods for sale.
11 Opportunity for role play.

Materials

1   Purses, handbags, shopping baskets; in matched sets for size and colour or fabric.
2   Real money, cash register or till.
3   Scales.
4   Notepads for cashiers' and shoppers' lists.
5   Materials for posters, labels and advertisements.
6   Real groceries (loaned from home for short periods and returned) and goods for shops.
7   Dressing-up clothes for waitresses and hairdressers.

8   Cashiers' stamps for bank.
9   Shop goods made by the children.

Cooking
Our observations in schools suggest that cooking is becoming an isolated activity, separated from the children's play. This is especially the case when mothers are given the responsibility of supervising 'the cooking group'. It often has no connection with any other school activity, except perhaps mathematics and reading. The results are handed around to children in the class, to teachers and visitors in the staffroom, or taken home to be eaten.

We appreciate that some schools have no facilities for cooking, but teachers are aware of many recipes that are suitable for children that do not require the use of a cooker. Also there are books containing such recipes simple enough for children to read. Some schools are assisted by parents, grandparents or friends who live nearby and will cook the children's 'goodies' at home. Even where there is a cooker it is advisable to include in the recipes some that require no cooking, so that when children are playing without an adult involved they can still prepare real dishes in safety.

When mothers are supervising they often do not know the reason for their presence, i.e. that after one or two sessions when the children have been helped they should be able to use the recipe and complete the cooking on their own. Mothers often underestimate the children and give too much assistance, not realizing, for instance, that infants are quite able to separate the yolk of an egg from the white. If the recipe calls for an action beyond their capability then it is too difficult, and should be left for older children to use later. When joining in the children's cooking, one is initiating them into the mysteries of real cooking so that in their play they can cook and eat the results if they wish. Nevertheless the same children will sometimes still play 'pretend cooking' and make cakes, scones, or dinners with sand, leaves or flour and salt dough.

Birthday parties
Children often play at birthday parties when they have pretend meals so we are suggesting ways in which play can be incorporated with cooking, in order that the children become familiar with the inclusion of real cooking in domestic play.

The teacher needs to observe domestic play and, when the children are playing parties, to discuss with them all the preparations that are necessary, remembering that some of them may not have experienced a party. First it must be decided how many children will come to the party and the children can then prepare the invitations. If possible they could go to a card shop to look at ready-made invitations. Failing this, some examples could be brought in for the children to examine and discuss. Having consulted the calendar for the date, and decided on the time, the invitations can be illustrated, written and, if there is a school or class post-box, posted and later delivered. Any last-minute invitations can be telephoned. The next discussion concerns the menu; once this has been agreed and the recipes selected, shopping lists are written. Again if possible an expedition to the local shops follows with an adult, and the necessary purchases are made. If outside visits are impossible the necessary ingredients can be put into the classroom shop.

Back in school, the utensils needed for the cooking are prepared and the ingredients set out. Reading the recipe, measuring, weighing, counting and timing will be involved. It will be necessary to ensure that hands and cooking surfaces are clean and that equipment is stored cleanly and tidily after it has been used.

While the food is cooking or setting, the remaining preparations for the party take place. Paper hats may be made, place cards written and decorated, paper serviettes made and folded, doilies shaped and patterned, cardboard plates cut and decorated and the tables set. Some children may wish to wear party clothes from the dressing-up box as well as their party hats.

After the meal, party games can be planned and prepared for. 'Pass the parcel', 'Blind man's buff', 'Pass the ring on a string' may be new experiences for some children. A visit to the cinema or watching the television are often today's party activities! When the party is over and the guests have left, the tidying up and washing up remain to be done.

Once children have experienced an extended play situation like this they may repeat and adapt it on future occasions, often inviting an adult to participate and using only the aspects they choose or remember. Obviously the play described would be extended over more than one day, and an adult closely involved in the first instance; she would always ask for the children's suggestions to advance the play. After a teacher has initiated these advances on the children's original party play a nursery nurse or welfare assistant could take over and be involved in the play on another occasion if requested.

Examples of motivation, learning and development that may occur in this play

1 Social interaction between children and adults.
2 Language. In this kind of play language is used for reasoning: 'You have to stir it a lot to get rid of the lumps.'

Children report on their actions often recalling their past experience: 'I'm pouring it in slowly. Luke poured his quickly and made it too runny.'

They direct the actions of others: 'Shake it through the sieve like this. Now rub the crumbs that are left with the spoon. Watch me.'

They maintain their rights in the play: 'It's not your turn yet. I'm second. I'm next after him.'

They predict the results of their actions: 'If you forget to put the sugar in no one will eat it.'

They may project the feelings of others: 'If she touches that it'll burn and it'll hurt her and she'll cry.'

3 New vocabulary needed: palette knife, spatula, granulated, caster sugar, beat in, fold in, sieve, simmer, scour.
4 Mathematical concepts: counting, measuring, weighing, using money, measuring time.
5 Scientific concepts in mixing and cooking.
6 Manipulative skills, e.g. in cooking.
7 Practice in observation, e.g. examining invitation cards.
8 Motivation and practice in reading and writing.
9 Motivation to use books, e.g. for recipes.
10 Concentration and application in completing tasks.
11 Realization of the need for cleanliness in cooking.

Materials

1 Writing, drawing, painting, collage materials, scissors.
2 Recipe books, possibly for teacher to copy for children to read.
3 Cooking equipment – full size but small and light enough for children to handle: bowl, basins, measuring jug, different sized spoons, spatula, palette knife, baking tin, cake cases, saucepans, scales and weights.
4 Washing and cleaning equipment: dishcloths, glasscloths, dish-mop, pan scourer, washing-up liquid.
5 Cookery timer, tape measure or string for head measurement.

Cleaning

The rapidity with which children often perform cleaning tasks in domestic play suggests that they sometimes lack the equipment to do a satisfactory job, and that very often the domestic play is too confined to allow them to move about. When the teacher joins in the domestic play she can help the children examine the equipment, and discuss spring cleaning. Together they can decide the sequence of the work and the tools and materials required. Children will have many suggestions to make and will be inspired to take a pride in caring for the furniture and equipment. They will play more imaginatively in the future. The work could be divided into:

sweeping: shelves, floor, carpets
polishing: furniture, floor, shoes
dusting: furniture, ornaments
washing: walls, tables, chairs, dolls' beds, shelves, curtains, cushion covers, tablecloths, bed covers, dolls' clothes and, after all the work is completed, cloths and dusters.

When the teacher is helping the children to organize an extended cleaning session the play may well last two or three days. Subsequently, when the children are playing, their cleaning in the house will have profited by this. They will be familiar with the use of the equipment, know that it is provided and where it is stored in the classroom. Although children have seen cleaning utensils used in the home and have imitated what they have seen, their observation may be incomplete and they may not have realized how the equipment is used, for example, they may not know which way to tip the dustpan in order to collect the dust, or how much polish to put on shoes. Unless they have the opportunity to use polish, detergents, soap, they do not understand their properties and cannot assess the amount needed for the job. At home they may not be allowed to use such materials. Equipment, tools and materials should be large enough to enable the children to perform their task satisfactorily. Guidance should be given in the storage and cleaning of tools and equipment, and *all* children need to know where materials are, so that all can share fully in this play. So often the girls are asked to tidy the house rather than the boys; obviously they are more competent if the boys never have the chance to practise!

Examples of motivation, learning and development that may occur in this type of play
1 Cooperation and social interaction between children.
2 Cooperation with an adult and realization that this play is valued.

3   Language. Many opportunities occur in this play when children use language to reason: 'Look, if you sweep the dirt up near the wall how can I get the pan down so's you can sweep it into the dustpan?'

As they clean ·they report on their experiences: 'Last time I did the washing up I put a cup on there where it was wet and it slipped off and broke.'

They talk about their imaginary situation: 'I'm hurrying up with the housework because I'm going to visit my friend this afternoon.'

There are many opportunities to direct their peers: 'Rub harder than that or else it won't shine much.'

Self-maintaining language is frequently necessary: 'I'll empty the water. I'm best at it. I can do it without spilling a drop. You always make a mess on the floor.'

Children predict the result of their actions: 'I mustn't put too much polish on. It won't come shiny if I do, even if I rub ever so hard.'

They project into the reactions of others: 'When the teacher sees how shiny this is she'll be saying "You've made it look like a palace".'

4   New vocabulary needed: dry surface, dilute, film of polish/dust, sparkle, reflection, concentrated powder, inflammable, do not puncture, destroy after use, detergent.

5   Mathematical: ordering, stacking and storing of cleaning equipment, mops, brushes, cloths, dusters.

6   Scientific: sequence of cleaning activities, e.g. don't sweep after having dusted, sweep walls before floors, too much polish dulls surfaces. Washing, shrinking, and stretching of curtains or covers.

7   Manipulative skill in using tools and equipment.

8   Experience of sound: scrape, scrub, squeak.

9   Reading: instructions on materials, e.g. 'Shake well before use'.

10 Writing: 'Do not remove', 'Please don't touch until dry'.

11 Motivation to observe adults and to imitate their skill.

Materials

1   Dusters, floor cloths, squeegee mop.

2   Handbrush and pan, sweeping brush, carpet sweeper, Hoover.

3   Bucket, bowl.

4   Polish, scouring powder.

5   Warm water.

Washing

Many schools now provide model washing machines and sink units for the children's pretend play. These stimulate imaginative play. But there is a difference in the play that occurs when water is available and when children are able to wash up after a birthday party or to wash dusters and cloths after a cleaning session. The play is prolonged and gives rise to conversation, encourages care in the handling of equipment, promotes physical and manipulative skill and develops learning situations.

The teacher can discuss with the children how to separate the washing into wool, cotton, nylon, coloureds or whites. They can see how much longer woollens take to dry than nylon. They can sort the materials that need ironing and iron them with the house corner iron and ironing board. Some teachers working with the Project have provided irons that have been 'doctored' to remain at 'cool' heat.

Very few of the Project teachers had no water in their classrooms. But even where there is no sink in the room, water can be brought in and kept in a container. This gives the children valuable experience in pouring, filling utensils and carrying water.

An important part of house play is keeping the materials clean and attractive. When the dressing-up clothes, bed clothes and dolls' clothes are dirty, torn and creased, it is not surprising if domestic play is unproductive of imaginative and learning situations. It is not the teacher's or mother's job to mend, wash or tidy these things, this is an important part of domestic play which the children should enjoy and not be denied.

Note: We hope readers do not have the unfortunate experience one of the Project teachers had. She was demonstrating how wool shrinks when put in very hot water; in her case it stretched!

Ways in which this play could be developed

1   Visits to the supermarket to compare all the different washing powders and soap.
2   Visits to the launderette with the school laundry, e.g. library cushion cases.
3   Experiments in washing different garments to measure shrinkage.
4   Experiments to compare dye, colour fastness.
5   Experiments to compare lengths of time taken in drying.
6   Experiments to discover solvent properties of soap, soap flakes, detergents.
7   Collections of different types of fabrics.
8   Comparison of advertisement slogans for washing powders and soaps.

9 Inventing slogans for washing powders and fabrics.
10 Comparison of different types of washing machines.
11 Measurement of capacity of water used in hand washing, clothes washing.
12 Discovery of launderette consumption of water.
13 Reading washing labels on clothes.
14 Reading and listening to stories about washday.
15 Making books about washing clothes and going to the launderette.
16 Fabric printing, tie-dyeing, simple weaving.

Examples of motivation, learning and development that may occur in this play

1 Social: need to cooperate.
2 Language. Children use language to reason when they wash: 'I'm putting a lot of soap on here because this is where the dirt is.'

They report their previous experience as they describe their actions: 'When I was watching my mum she did it like this so I'm shaking the tin first too.'

When they use language to imagine they may also draw on their experience, possibly from TV advertisements as in this example: 'I'm using this to make my woollens soft and springy. Then my little girl will say "Ooh Mum my cardigan feels lovely and cuddly".'

Sometimes their 'directing' language is aimed at themselves: 'Teacher said "Don't put too much soap powder in the water. It's expensive".'

When children play together there are nearly always occasions for self-maintaining language: 'I have to peg the clothes on the line. I'm the biggest. You can hold the basket.'

Predictions are often necessary: 'Don't put it back in the soapy water. We'll have to rinse it again if you do.'

Children project into the reactions of adults, often making them respond in the way they would like: 'When the teacher sees how clean those are she'll be very pleased.'

3 New vocabulary needed: weak/strong solution, pummel, smooth, wrinkle, texture, tumble dry, evaporate, synthetic, man-made fibre, artificial, trickle, gurgle, detergent.
4 Mathematical concepts: measuring detergents, water, cost of soap and soap powder, capacity.

5 Scientific concepts: dissolving, drying, evaporating, shrinking, stretching, rinsing, bleaching, dyeing.
6 Manipulative skill: pouring, squeezing, rubbing, pegging, ironing.
7 Sound experience as water splashes, trickles, rushes and gurgles.
8 Aesthetic: pattern, colour, texture.
9 Motivation to read.
10 Concentration and effort involved.
11 Hygiene: need for cleanliness.

Materials
1 Bowl, bath, sink, washing machines.
2 Iron and ironing board.
3 Spin/tumble dryer, wringer.
4 'Maiden', clothes airer (horse), clothes line, pegs, laundry basket, coat-hangers.
5 Soap, detergent, soap powder measurer.

House furnishing and decorating
These are the days of 'do it yourself' in the home. Most children have experience of parents making furniture and furnishing and decorating rooms. For many small boys this may be how they identify their father's role and the only way they can imitate him in domestic play. We must provide the chance for children to make and use household equipment. So often we succumb to our own liking for the perfect finished article that will last, and deprive the children of the motivation and learning experience of making their own.

If wood and wooden boxes are not easily available or are too difficult for younger children to work with, large cardboard boxes and containers are readily available. These boxes can be fastened together with strips of gummed paper or magazines to make them more solid. Cupboards, dressers, cookers, washing machines and dishwashers can be constructed and painted. They may not last as long as those from the educational suppliers but they are very satisfying to the children and provide excellent language, reading, writing and mathematical experience. Children are encouraged to look closely at and study their furniture and equipment at home. They will ask questions and interest their parents in their play. In one Project school a class of older infants made a bathroom and lavatory suite to extend their house play; they constructed kitchen, dining and sitting room furniture, all from cardboard boxes. When this 'do it yourself' furniture has disintegrated, the motivation to make it again and improve on the first time will be there because the children use the end-products. They can understand why chairs have to be well made and exactly measured.

Some schools make their own houses. The bricks are made from shoe boxes or similar sized boxes which the children cover and paint. When a roof, windows and door are added, many mathematical and construction problems have to be solved. Wallpaper is made from the children's patterns or symmetry experiments and the walls are covered. There is as much measuring and matching of patterns, shape and size when this is done as there is in covering the table or dresser in the house. How often does the teacher or teacher's aide cover or paint table-tops, boxes and shelves herself! Why can't the children learn to do it?

Many soft furnishings are required for domestic play. As girls may enjoy making furniture, so some boys find pleasure in making and sewing fabrics. Curtains, tablecloths, bedcovers and cushion covers are all simple enough for children to make with the minimum of assistance. If sewing is not possible material can be stapled. Instructions can be written out for them to follow once they have measured the windows and furniture.

There is an added interest in tie-dyeing and fabric printing if they are going to make something they want. Books, magazines and diagrams will need to be consulted. A detailed record can be kept of the progress of the house furnishing. Stories about houses can also be written. Visits to the nearest 'do it yourself' store must be made, so that the children can examine and, if need be, purchase handles and fastenings.

Teachers can analyse the play that has just been described for the motivation, learning and development. Our analysis can be found in Appendix 1.

Materials
1 Wood, wooden boxes, woodwork bench and tools, nails, screws, glue.
2 Cardboard boxes and containers, extra-strong stapler, scissors.
3 Fabrics, cotton, wool, needles.
4 Paper, card, paint, brushes.
5 Junk materials for decoration.

6 Fabric printing equipment.
7 Books, magazines, diagrams, catalogues.
8 Reading and writing materials.

Hospitals

Even if a child-sized bed is not provided children will improvise one in order to play at going to bed and being ill. They all have experience of illness and visiting the doctor, and if they have not been in hospital have usually seen hospitals portrayed on the television or in films. Some children's hospitals allow parties from school to visit in order to familiarize children with hospitals. Such visits provide many experiences that are used in play later. The teacher can provide bandages, Elastoplast, discarded plaster casts, medicine measures, syringes. She can help the children to make nurses' and doctors' uniforms and masks. Medical instruments are improvised from water play or other science equipment and medicine from orangeade, lemonade and raspberryade. Plastic beakers and measures avoid the danger of breakages; children need bottles and tubes to set up blood transfusion units, for example. There are many books that the children read that give them new ideas for the play. The teacher's help may be required initially to work out diet charts, temperature charts and visiting hours, but the children should be able to continue the play by themselves. Similarly they may need help to arrange appointment records and treatment cards for an outpatients' department.

At times when the hospital play has become popular it will be necessary to provide much more space than usual. At least two beds are needed to make a ward and still more space for visits and the hospital staff. If an outpatients, X-ray and casualty department are also required it may be necessary to spill over into the corridor or hall. Where the classroom is the only room available the teacher may well feel that enough children and sufficient reading, writing, mathematical and scientific concepts are involved to warrant using most of the classroom space as long as the hospital interest lasts. The children need to write lists, notices, make patients' records, develop new language, weigh and measure their patients, understand capacity for injections and medicine dosage, allocate time for appointments, read notices and instructions and cooperate.

The class shops and post office can be incorporated in Hospital Play. Get-well cards can be made, purchased, written, posted and delivered. Gifts such as books or toys can be made and sold in the shops to hospital visitors.

Some children may be more familiar with the baby clinic or the doctor's surgery. They may want to weigh and measure dolls and issue baby food. Once again posters and instruction charts can be made by the children and records kept. Experience of the doctor's group practice or clinic may lead to the need for a 'waiting room', appointments desk and Sister's surgery for injections, plaster and bandaging. It will most certainly require a telephone, and the doctor may need to visit patients at home.

Teachers can analyse the play that has just been described for the motivation, learning and development. Our analysis can be found in Appendix 1.

Materials
1   Child-sized beds, bedcovers.
2   Nurses' and doctors' clothes, clinical masks.
3   Stethoscope, syringe, thermometer.
4   Medicine bottles, spoons, beakers, spatulas, tubing.
5   Bandages, plasters, plaster cast.
6   Scales – child-sized, baby-sized, measuring chart.
7   Books, cards, paper, clipboards.
8   Telephone.
9   Crockery, cutlery.
10   Sink, washing equipment.
11   Bench, cupboard, boxes to make desk or counter.
12   Junk materials to improvise all of these.

Using Domestic Play
1   Provide in turn for the eight different kinds of domestic play described, paying particular attention to any which does not occur in your classroom.
2   Remember to discuss this with the children and take the cues from them.
3   Observe the play as often as possible and record the learning and development.

5 Construction Play

Introduction

In Construction Play we analyse the motivation, learning and development in each description of play as before and now ask the question 'How did the teacher structure the play?' The analysis of the last description of play and the questions are left for the teachers to answer. Our analyses can be found in Appendix 1.

Stimuli

The descriptions of construction play are listed under the stimuli from which they arose:

1   first-hand experience in the home
2   a story
3   the environment
4   a television programme.

In the following pages we describe the children referring to books, pictures, diagrams and the real construction. We would beg all teachers to remember that the final results are children's own constructions, a skilled teacher has merely made suggestions in the first place. There is a danger that adults may expect the children's constructions to be too realistic or perfectly formed. We cannot impose adult standards in the children's play; their building will often appear ramshackle, unfinished and unrepresentational to our eyes, yet it is very satisfying to the children, much more so than our polished perfected intention.

Space

Plenty of room is needed for both large and small construction play. If space is severely restricted a teacher might consider providing for construction play only on certain days when she limits other play. This will give more floor space for large constructions. If noise is a problem with large bricks, it is a good idea to let the building take place on a carpeted area; young children need to break down a construction and even older children will have crashes. It should be remembered that constructions made with small materials like Sticklebricks and Lego can need a large space and can be extensive. They should not always be confined to a small space or to a small table. They may need floor space or a large bench or table if they are to be very imaginative, or comprise more than one construction, e.g. not one aeroplane but several combined with air terminals.

Some teachers have reported that small construction play, for example with Lego, was often solitary and non-cooperative. This may be because space was restricted. Large extensive constructions are more likely to give rise to cooperation. They encourage the children to combine their constructions and take part in cooperative, imaginative play. Of course all construction play need not be cooperative or require a great deal of space, but restricted space may mean restricted play and confined imagination.

In fine weather, if access is easy, construction play can be moved outside, thus solving the twin problems of space and noise.

Materials

Construction materials are equally attractive to young and older infants. But a variety of materials are needed to ensure that the manipulative skills of all children are given the opportunity to develop. Materials must be large and small, heavy and light, varied in shape and texture. Children find the materials adaptable: a large box can be the base of a tower or a dog kennel; a Kugeli construction can become an octopus in an undersea drama or a space ship.

The following materials were found in the majority of the Project schools. We therefore presume they are within the normal school budget:

Bricks: wooden, plastic, interlocking.
Barrels, planks, tubs, cubes, boxes with and without wheels, cardboard and wooden boxes.
Junior Engineer, Timbabuild, Lego, Meccano, Kugeli.
Small bricks and wooden or plastic shapes.
Constructostraws, Playplax, Sticklebricks, Poleidoblocks, Tinkertoy.
Train sets, railroad layout, harbour, road plan layout, farm buildings, dolls' houses.
Miniature cars, boats, animals, soldiers, dolls.

String, glue, nails, woodwork tools, fabrics, newspaper and staplers will be required for making many constructions.

Storage

Storage of construction materials is very important. Here are some suggestions:

1 Bookshelves or open cupboard shelves can be used for storing large planks and wooden building shapes; frequently these will

only fit in one way which the children learn and which gives excellent practice in the formation of spatial concepts.

2 A large chest or box possibly on wheels into which the materials will fit in only one way can store different kinds of construction materials.

3 Shelves or a box which necessitate the children matching the shapes so that all of one shape or size or colour go on one shelf or in one box.

4 Smaller bricks can often be stacked carefully inside large cubes and space saved in this way.

5 Planks may be up-ended in barrels, so may tubes of cardboard or rolls of corrugated card.

6 Smaller cardboard boxes can be tidily stacked inside larger ones.

If the materials are not easily available the children will not use them. If they are not easily stored away, they will shirk the job.

Stimulus: First-hand experience in the home
(Play with small bricks and wooden shapes)

One teacher observed that Warren, aged five, was very involved in building with small bricks and shapes. In a spot check she noticed that he had been making the same construction for fifteen minutes. When she went to talk with him about his building he told her he was making a cupboard like the one his father had made for his bedroom. He talked freely about sharing the bedroom with his brother, and about the other furniture his father had made for the house. Three other children joined in the conversation, discussing what kind of furniture was needed in a bedroom and the kitchen fitments another father had made.

Jenny and Marianne found a shoe box that they wanted to fit out and a mother helping in the classroom volunteered to look through some magazines with them. They talked at length about sink units, broom cupboards, working tops, and the need to use all the available space. The girls then cooperated to build the fitments for their kitchen in their shoe box!

Meanwhile Warren had continued to make his bedroom furniture. He made a chest of drawers and then announced that he wanted to make a dressing table to match his cupboard which he was now calling a wardrobe. The same mother helped him to study a mail order catalogue and talked about the pictures of wardrobe cum dressing table units. As a result Warren completed his bedroom furniture taping tinfoil round a brick to make the mirror for his dressing table.

Ian, who had been the fourth member to join the discussion group, wanted to make bookshelves like some that had recently been fixed in the corridor to take the overflow from the school library. Many of the boys in the class had talked to the carpenter when he was working. At the teacher's suggestion Ian went to study the shelves carefully and came back to tell her that he was going to make his with one big shelf to take the tall books. She then helped him to reason that it was better to have the heaviest books on the bottom shelf. He used Cuisenaire rods to make the shelves and carefully fitted different sized bricks to represent the books in the completed bookcase.

Examples of motivation, learning and development that occurred in this play

1   Shared interest with at least one adult.
2   Cooperation between two girls.
3   Language. The children used language in many ways when they discussed their play with the adults or talked to themselves as they built.

They reasoned as they selected the size and shape they needed: 'That one won't go in there, it's too long and the wrong shape.'

They reported from their home experience: 'My mum says you must have somewhere inside the cupboard doors to hang your saucepan lids.'

They imagined as they discussed and constructed: 'What colour shall we have for our sink unit? I think yellow would look nice. Do you like yellow in a kitchen?'

They gave directions to each other as they cooperated: 'Put that little brick in there while I hold this one up.'

They maintained their position in the group: 'No, I don't want that colour for the shelves. You're making the sink unit. I'm doing the cupboards so I can choose the colour for the shelves.'

They predicted the results of their actions: 'If I put a big book in there it will knock this shelf down.'

They projected into the reactions of others: 'The people won't like it if they can't put any big books in the library.'
4   New vocabulary needed: chest of drawers, tallboy, corner fitment, double sink unit, waste disposal unit, collapsible ironing board, mixer tap, eye-level grill, catalogue, index, scale drawing.
5   Practice in matching shapes, size and colour.

6 Practice in spatial concepts, e.g. fitting bricks and shapes together in a cardboard box.
7 Practice in careful observation: difference in depth of shelves.
8 Manipulative skill in fixing bricks and shapes.
9 Practice in looking carefully at pictures.
10 Realization that reference can be made to real objects, e.g. library bookshelves.
11 Motivation for the first boy to observe his father carefully and for the other children to relate the discussion to their own experience.
12 Realization that reference can be made to books and magazines.
13 Concentration and application resulting from the self-motivation, the availability and attractiveness of the materials, the encouragement of an adult and the suitability of the task, i.e. it was within their capability yet presented problems and called for skill.
14 Motivation for future play resulting from a self-chosen task successfully completed, difficulties overcome, and the value attached to their play by their peers and the adults around.

HOW DID THE TEACHER STRUCTURE THIS PLAY?
1 By providing:
   (a) a variety of bricks and construction materials
   (b) a variety of junk materials
   (c) magazines, catalogues and books.
2 By involvement.

How did the teacher become involved?
1 She observed the play.
2 She showed interest.
3 She initiated a discussion.
4 She invited the assistance of parent-helpers.

Why did the teacher become involved?
1 The first boy was a new entrant who did not join in other children's play but played on his own with the small bricks. The teacher wanted to encourage him to talk to her and to others in the class.
Objective: to establish a relationship with a newcomer and help him to develop his self-image as a recognized member of the class.
2 She realized that 'do it yourself' fitments would be a discussion topic many of the children could join in.
Objective: to interest other children in the class in solving problems in this construction play; to introduce other children

to the possibilities of incorporating their home experience of 'do it yourself' into their play.

3   She wanted to involve the parents in the classroom play and knew this was an interest they shared. The mothers would find their knowledge was required; they would not be merely observing or encouraging.

Objective: to use mothers willing to help in the class in a purposeful way; to show mothers how much learning and development occurs in construction play.

Other extensions of the play that might have followed with the help of a teacher

1   Drawing and painting or making collages of the furniture for a bedroom, library or kitchen.
2   Making scale drawings of fitments and furniture.
3   Writing about their own constructions, about libraries, bedrooms, kitchens or other rooms in the house. Making books of furniture and furnishings. Compiling kitchen or bedroom catalogues with illustrations either of their own or cut from magazines or catalogues.
4   Compiling lists of names of furniture and furnishings for different rooms (possibly classified alphabetically or in some other way devised by the children) and making sets of wood, metal and other materials.

Other kinds of play based on the same stimulus

It happened that this play originated from a construction made with small bricks. It could equally well have developed from a construction with large bricks or boxes and planks, or from cardboard boxes or one made at the woodwork bench. Similarly it could have been developed into building large furniture for Domestic Play as described previously.

A similar play activity observed in an SPA school concerned two girls aged seven; no other small building materials being available, they were playing at a bench using discarded Cuisenaire rods. They had made an elaborate plan of rooms and corridors which in discussion with an adult they identified as a block of flats with launderette, lift, playground and pram store. They were called away to an exciting balloon race and when they returned, their interest was lost. Nevertheless if they had not been disturbed one can see how this play could have been developed, calling on these children's rich experience of living in a large block of new flats.

A much younger boy in a reception group in a village school was making a rabbit hutch from Lego because he had just been given a rabbit for which his father and brother had built a hutch. Discussion with the teacher and with a small group of children led to his building other animal houses and playing with model farm animals in his constructions. Later, with the teacher's assistance, he wrote and illustrated a book about animal houses.

Stimulus: A story
(Play with small bricks and blocks)
A few days after she had read the story of *The Little House* to a class of six and seven year olds the teacher heard a group discussing their buildings. Two boys and two girls were playing with a variety of wooden bricks on a table. Judith said she was making the little house just like it was in the story. Wendy offered to help by making the fence for the garden. Eamon and Edward announced that they were building houses too. This caused an argument; the girls maintained that there was only one little house and that they were building it. The boys were frustrated because there was not enough room to build several houses on the table. The teacher intervened to suggest that they take their building materials into the hall, and to remind them about the skyscrapers that were erected around the little house. The children transferred their play to the hall where they surrounded the little house with shops, hotels, skyscraper blocks, offices and a maze of roads.

The next day they wanted to continue their play in the hall. Eamon and Edward took in miniature cars and lorries to move along the roads and Judith said she would soon have to move her little house away from the skyscrapers. Eamon had forgotten this part of the story, so the teacher suggested Wendy should find the book in the library and read it aloud to the group. Edward suggested that the girls bring the farm equipment from the classroom and set up a farm on the opposite side of the hall. The girls did this while the boys continued to build skyscrapers and play with police cars, ambulances and lorries.

When Judith announced that the new site was ready all four children combined for the removal. At their first attempt to lift the house it collapsed. They rebuilt it amidst the skyscrapers and began to discuss how they could lift it on to a transporter. By this time the teacher was involved in the play. She joined in to help them rebuild the little house and talked to them about her life in Canada and how she had seen houses removed and resited there. Eamon said he didn't know you could move houses like that, he thought you had to take them to pieces like they did when they took London Bridge to America. He told them he'd been talking to his dad about it the previous night. Edward said his uncle had a trailer at the back of his car to fasten his motor bike on when he went to rallies, and perhaps they could make a trailer to put the little house on. Wendy argued that they'd still got to lift the house on to the trailer and that was when it collapsed last time. Eamon talked at length about a grab he had watched picking up old cars that were being demolished. All the group remembered seeing this on the television. Wendy said her nan had told her that men had lifted their car on to the boat like this years ago when they had taken it to France. Edward laughed and said you drove your car on to a car ferry now. Judith argued that they would have to think of another way of lifting the little house on to the trailer because a grab would break it to pieces again. The teacher was participating in this discussion but leaving the suggestions to the children. She provided books and magazines when she thought they would help.

Eamon had brought the transporter along the road to the little house meanwhile and he and Edward had built a ramp that slanted from the trailer to the base of the house. Judith and Wendy contrived to slide a thick piece of cardboard under the large brick that formed the foundation for the little house, and had supported it with a large brick at the back. They were then able to push and pull the card gently up the sloping ramp and successfully moved the house on to the transporter. With great glee they transported the little house to its new site alongside the farm house and animals they had prepared for it.

Examples of motivation, learning and development that occurred in this play

1 Cooperating in building and reconstructing a shared experience with other children and with an adult.
2 Sharing a discussion with other children and an adult.
3 Language. The children used language in many ways among themselves as they were building and in discussion with their teacher. They reasoned: 'I'll have to make the base bigger or my skyscraper will topple over. It's too tall.'

   They reported to each other as they recalled the story: 'No, you can't put that there. There weren't any houses at first, only the little house. You'll have to put trees there.'

They imagined events that had not been recorded in the story: 'Ee-ow, ee-ow, here's an ambulance coming and a police car, there's an accident in the road in front of the little house.'

They gave directions to each other: 'Bring the transporter over here, move it round, see if we can get the house on this way.'

They maintained their right to property: 'Don't touch that brick, that's mine. I'm going to put it on this roof.'

They predicted the result of their actions: 'If we lift it up like that we won't get the wheels underneath, there isn't room.'

They projected into the intentions of the new owners of the little house: 'They're going to move the little house because they want it to be happy and they like living in the country too.'

4 New vocabulary needed: truck, elevator, conveyor, transporter, articulated vehicle, erect, excavate, hod, trowel, scaffolding, shuttering, hoist, architect, surveyor, plumb-bob, basement, storey, penthouse, sidewalk.

5 Selecting the correct size, shape and weight of materials.

6 Estimating the comparative size of skyscrapers and the little house.

7 Acquiring skill in manipulating materials.

8 Solving the problem of transporting the house.

9 Observing buildings in the environment carefully.

10 Observing illustrations in books carefully.

11 Recalling the events and their sequence in the story.

12 Selecting the most suitable materials.

HOW DID THE TEACHER STRUCTURE THIS PLAY?

1 By providing:
   (a) the extra space for building in the hall
   (b) the time for the play to be continued for two days
   (c) a combination of construction materials
   (d) a story that encouraged construction play
   (e) books and pictures of buildings, cities and transporter lorries.

2 By involvement.

How did the teacher become involved?

1 She told the story that gave rise to the play.

2 She intervened to suggest the children move into the hall.

3 She initiated the construction of the buildings that enveloped the little house.

4 She participated in the play to discover what were the problems in

lifting the house on to the transporter lorry.

5 She shared the children's discussions about lifting and transporting the little house.

Why did the teacher become involved?

1 These were seven year old children whom the teacher knew to be capable of building a more complicated construction than one little house. She saw the possibilities for play that could develop from the story.

Objective: to encourage the children to extend their play, meet problems and concentrate over a longer period.

2 She wanted to encourage the children to consult books and knew that there were many allied to this topic in the class and school libraries.

Objective: to motivate the children to incorporate into their play the skills and knowledge they already possessed; to motivate them to acquire new skills and knowledge in order to further their play.

3 When the children met the problem of lifting the little house, she observed that they were about to acknowledge defeat. She knew if they persevered and discovered what the problem was, they were capable of working out a solution.

Objective: to prove to the children that effort, perseverance and concentration are needed to overcome difficulties; to give the children the satisfaction of solving their own problem.

Other extensions of the play that might have followed with the help of a teacher

1 Excursions around the neighbourhood to look at different kinds of houses and shops.

2 A traffic count.

3 Observation on a building site.

4 Collections of pictures of houses and buildings, possibly classified, e.g. domestic, commercial, town, country.

5 Making collages, friezes, pictures of local streets and shops.

6 Writing stories and compiling books, self-illustrated or with pictures from magazines.

7 Building model houses with home-made bricks.

8 Mixing mortar, measuring constituents.

9 Inventing fantastic houses and buildings, e.g. on the moon or a strange planet or in the future.

10 Estimating time taken for a little house to be enveloped by large buildings.

Stimulus: The environment

I   AN EXPEDITION

(Play with large cardboard containers, planks, wooden boxes and bricks)

Four reception age boys had been taken on a short rail journey by a student and nursery nurse. The next day they were playing in the hall with a collection of large cardboard containers, wooden planks and shapes and two boxes on wheels which were used for storing bricks. When the nursery nurse noticed that they were using the wheeled boxes as a train she joined in their play. The cardboard containers were built up to form the ticket office and the ticket collector's shelter, the planks and bricks were used as the platform, and the blocks were placed inside the boxes for seats. Dressing-up clothes were brought for the ticket collector, guard and driver, and later in the week a Wendy house frame was made into a refreshment bar where lemonade, cups of tea, biscuits and cakes were sold.

'The nursery nurse decided that to join in with the play was the best way to initiate new developments.'

The play continued for several days and children who had not been on the original rail trip joined in. Many books about trains and journeys were looked at and stories read, and the original group made a record in book form of their excursion. The nursery nurse provided refreshments and made notices for the station that the children could recognize.

Examples of motivation, learning and development that occurred in this play

1 Shared experience with adults and other children, both in real life and the play situation.
2 Language. Because these were young children, many of the uses of language were introduced by the nursery nurse. She encouraged them to imagine, predict and project when she participated in their play.

The children used language for reasoning: 'That box is going to fall 'cos it isn't on straight.'

They reported when they were encouraged to recall their experience: 'You have to give the man your ticket. He clips it and then gives it back to you.'

They gave directions to each other: 'You're the ticket collector. You didn't take my ticket.'

They were quick in self-maintenance: 'I'm getting on first. I'm the driver. The driver's always on first.'
3 New vocabulary needed: left luggage office, station master, porter, departure board, timetable, first class compartment, railway carriage, traveller, tourist office, information bureau, newspaper stall, refreshment room.
4 Manipulative skill in using materials.
5 Physical skill in constructing and moving equipment.
6 Reference to books and pictures.
7 Drawing, writing and reading.
8 Using materials imaginatively.
9 Motivation to concentrate and persevere because of the interest aroused by the excursion and the opportunity to relive experience in play.
10 Experience of a developed play situation that helped children to extend their experiences into future play situations.

HOW DID THE TEACHER STRUCTURE THIS PLAY?

1 By providing:
   (a) space, i.e. in the hall
   (b) time – allowing the play to extend over several days

(c) materials – dressing-up clothes, Wendy house frame, ingredients to make cakes and biscuits sold in the refreshment bar.
2 By providing the stimulus for play in organizing the rail journey.
3 By freeing the nursery nurse so that she could become involved in the play.

How was the nursery nurse involved in the play situation?
1 By observing the play and realizing that it could be related to the railway expedition.
2 By participating in the children's play: note that these were young children and that the nursery nurse thought the most acceptable way to be involved was by participation:
   (a) because she had shared the experience with them and therefore could easily enter into and be accepted in their imitative play
   (b) because she suspected a discussion would have interrupted the situation and was afraid it might have ended the play.
   She decided that to join in with the play was the best way to initiate new developments.
3 By incorporating into the situation all the experiences the children had on their rail excursion.

Why did the nursery nurse become involved in the play situation?
1 Because her observation revealed that the play concerned an experience she had shared.
   Objective: to show the children that adults value play.
2 Because she observed that the children were not recalling all the events they had experienced.
   Objective: to recall a shared experience by re-enacting it in play.
3 Because she realized that the children had insufficient play experience to use the cardboard boxes and Wendy house frame in their construction.
   Objective: to initiate the improvised use of materials in construction.
4 Because the children's language was restricted to brief commands and demands. By participating in the play she was able to introduce dialogue through the imaginary situation she created: 'Which platform must I go to for the London train? How long shall I have to wait for the next train? Where can I buy my ticket? How shall we arrange the sweets in the refreshment room? If we put these boxes here, what might happen? What should I do, I have lost my luggage?'

The nursery nurse also caused the children to recall and describe what had happened on their railway journey: 'What did you say when you bought the tickets? Did the ticket collector say anything to us? What happened when we got into the compartment?'

She helped them to predict what would happen in their construction play: 'If we put that box on top of that tin what do you think it will do? Let's try and see if it does.'

Objectives: to foster language development and reasoning.

5 Because the children had not developed the imaginative possibilities of their play. The nursery nurse was not sure if the children could extend their play beyond an imitative stage. By joining in she introduced an imaginary situation: going on holiday, visiting the refreshment bar, and misplacing her luggage.

Objective: to develop the children's play by introducing imaginative ideas.

6 Because the children were beginning to play together and she wanted to encourage them in cooperative play. The adult involved several children by asking questions such as: 'Who is the ticket collector? I want my ticket clipped.' 'Are you a porter, can you tell me which platform . . .?' 'Who will help us fix this?'

Objective: to foster social development.

7 Because she saw the opportunities for role play for the children. She encouraged the children to be passengers, or refreshment bar assistants.

Objective: to foster emotional and social development.

Other extensions of the play that might have followed with the help of an adult

1 Listening to stories of engines and railways.
2 Listening to poetry about trains.
3 Listening to music about trains and railways.
4 Visit to school by railway employee, possibly a parent.
5 Setting up a model railway track.

2 AN OUTSIDE VISIT: A LOCAL CONSTRUCTION SITE

(Play with bricks, cars and road layout)

Nigel, Dennis, Percy and Jim, seven year olds, in a school near a motorway, were playing with bricks and cars on an old carpet. They were developing a layout of roads for the cars and lorries to move along. When the welfare assistant joined in their play and conversation, they drew a complicated road plan on the carpet with chalk.

After further discussion about the nearby flyover (referred to as 'spaghetti junction') the children tried to build a flyover, and motorway access and exit roundabout system. Many experiments resulted in their incorporating a wooden rail set, which they built on the small bricks to make raised roadways. Nigel, who obviously had been on this section of the motorway many times, was the leader although the others made frequent suggestions and amended his proposals when necessary. The adult on this occasion merely joined in the discussion and prompted the children to pursue and solve their problems by leading questions. The teacher saw the completed layout and realizing the children's interest, brought into school during the following week large-scale drawings of motorway plans, some aerial photographs and a large map of the country's motorways showing exit and access junctions. This inspired the play which continued and developed over several days requiring so much space that it was removed to a wide corridor. On one day the cars and lorries were used for a motorway 'pile-up' and larger bricks were used as cones to redirect traffic and close lanes. A construction was also erected with the larger bricks, batteries, flex, torches and bulbs to represent a warning lights panel.

Examples of motivation, learning and development that occurred in this play

1 Opportunity to play out a possibly frightening or strange experience.
2 Cooperation between the children.
3 Language. The boys used language to reason: 'If you let cars come in to the roundabout from there will they crash into those coming from this road?'

   They used language to record as they recalled their own motoring experiences: 'We had to move over into this lane when we were getting near the café.'

   They used language to explain their imagining to each other: 'This car is coming along much too fast, he's going to crash into you. It'll be a motorway pile-up.'

   They issued directions: 'Stop at the toll bridge. He's taking the money.'

   They maintained their position in the play: 'I'm in the police car. If I flash my STOP sign you must pull in immediately.'

   They predicted the results of the actions of others in the group: 'If he puts a "Road Closed" sign there all the traffic will be held up on this side road.'

They projected into the reactions of the motorists: 'He's glad he's on the motorway now. He loves speeding, he pretends he's a racing driver.'

4 New vocabulary needed: subway, clearway, lane closed/restricted/reopened, obstructed, fog and early warning system, hard shoulder, service station, motorway regulations, highway code, flyover.

5 Reference to pictures, diagrams, books.

6 Reading was incorporated by studying the new road signs in use in their home town as well as on the motorway. *The Highway Code* was used and individual and group books made on traffic signs and road vehicles.

7 Mathematical: the children measured the mileage of the motorway on a large map, using the map scale, and discovering the system in numbering access and exit points. They worked out routes and mileage from their home town to places they had been to, or were going to for the holidays.

8 The children worked out a circuit for their warning lights panel.

9 They solved problems in construction.

10 They practised manipulative skill in making their constructions.

11 Motivation to observe surroundings.

12 Motivation to recall experience accurately.

HOW DID THE TEACHER STRUCTURE THIS PLAY?

1 By providing:

(a) sufficient floor space for the children to carry out their ideas. When the children were being frustrated by lack of space and their play was interfering with other children's activities, the teacher suggested that it be transferred to the corridor.

(b) time – the teacher enabled the play to continue over several days.

(c) materials for road layout. The children needed to combine different materials for this construction – model road vehicles, the rail set, bricks of different sizes, equipment for the warning lights panel.

(d) materials that would enable the children to understand the road system and have a bird's eye view. She brought maps and diagrams and aerial photographs.

(e) materials for reading, writing and drawing about the play. The teacher found books on road transport, road construction, road builders, and road regulations, e.g. toll bridges, ancient and modern. She provided books on means of transport in other lands – rickshaws, horses, elephants, bullock carts, and discussed what kind of roads they used.

(f) materials for mathematics and science in the play. The teacher provided string and rulers to measure mileage and bulbs and batteries and flex for the light panel. The children had seen other children in the class making a circuit for a lighthouse they had built earlier in the term.

(g) experience of construction. The children were frustrated in their initial failure to build a flyover with the rail set. They could not raise a section of it as they wished. After discussion and examining pictures they devised a method of balancing it on a brick foundation.

2 By involvement.

How did the teacher become involved?

1 By observing: to decide when was the opportune time to participate, intervene or initiate.

2 By participating.

3 By intervening: when she discovered the children were being frustrated in their attempts to build a flyover, the teacher discussed it with the children enabling them to identify the problem and to reason out possible solutions which they could then try out.

4 By initiating the removal to the corridor.

5 By helping the children to consult books, photographs, maps and diagrams.

6 By suggesting in discussion with the children possible extensions of their play, e.g. comparison of distance travelled on holidays and other excursions, imaginary accidents and other events necessitating road closures and diversions, the addition of an electrical circuit to the warning lights panel.

7 By discussing with the children the teacher encouraged them to recall their observations and experiences accurately and in logical sequence.

8 By discussing she led them to predict the consequences of their experiments in fixing the flyover structure, erecting road signs and devising the warning lights panel, e.g. 'If you put that there what do you think might happen to those cars?'

9 She encouraged them to explain why they were interpreting the photographs, maps and diagrams in certain ways and to discuss why the traffic and road symbols are designed as they are. She decided that joining in with the play was the best way to initiate new developments.

1 Because when she listened to the children's dialogue about the layout it was obvious that they were not clear what they were trying to evolve in their road plans.

   Objective: to enable the children to identify their problem and continue their play.

2 Because she observed the children's repeated failures when attempting to build a flyover. This was when she introduced a book and a picture of a flyover. The teacher was not sure if the children would be able to relate the two-dimensional picture to their construction but she gave them the opportunity to study the picture.

   Objective: to give the children information which would alleviate their frustration and enable them to solve their problem.

3 Because she knew the boys were sufficiently interested in their play to be motivated to consult books, photographs and plans.

   Objective: to show children that books could be useful and reading purposeful.

4 Because she realized the potential of the boys' dialogue for promoting their language development. They could be encouraged to recall events and observations accurately, to predict the results of their constructions, the movement of their model vehicles, and the erection of road signs and obstructions.

   Objective: to foster children's language development.

5 Because she knew the boys had the mathematical concepts that would enable them to understand the numbering of motorway interchanges, exit and access junctions, and to work out mileages.

   Objective: to foster children's mathematical development and provide reasons the child could understand for the need to measure and count accurately.

6 Because she knew the boys had observed other children set up an electrical circuit.

   Objective: to encourage children to recall and apply the scientific knowledge previously acquired.

7 Because she observed that the boys were reasoning and planning during their play.

   Objective: to develop the possibilities in this play situation for logical reasoning.

8 Because she valued the imaginative potential of the play situation and observed how the boys were developing their experience beyond the limitation of experience into imaginary journeys with accidents. She therefore joined in their play and helped them

recall events and predict outcomes.

Objective: to foster imaginative play.

9 Because she observed the cooperation necessitated by the play. She suggested ways in which the boys could combine as the play was extended, and introduced ideas that required joint activity.

Objective: to provide situations which cause social play and help the children to understand the value of cooperative play.

Other extensions of the play that might have followed with the help of a teacher

1 Collection of motoring rules.
2 Collection of road safety rules.
3 Visit by Police Road Safety Unit, and layout of roads, crossroads, pedestrian crossings, traffic lights in the playground.
4 Writing and making books about different vehicles in use on roads, particularly container vehicles.
5 Collage, painting, drawing, motorway figures or large pictures.
6 Visit and talk by road engineer or parent employed on motorway or as a long-distance driver.

Stimulus: A television programme

(Play with large interlocking plastic bricks)

John, Peter, David and Susan, all six years old, had built a three-sided construction against the wall of the classroom. One member of the group in turn was shut inside the walls, which were raised if the next person was taller than the previous one.

When the teacher talked to the children it became clear that they had all watched an episode of the television series *Colditz* the previous evening. She intervened because the play seemed to have reached stalemate and the children did not know what to do once they had built the walls as high as the tallest child.

The discussion revealed that the children had been especially interested in the escape methods used by the prisoners of war in Colditz prison. They volunteered many examples from previous episodes they had viewed. The children tried several times to build the prison so that a hole could be made in one wall without causing the wall to collapse, and then to build it so that a tunnel could be made underneath. The problem was solved with the teacher's help by moving the site to the other side of the room and joining their construction to a play house. They built their walls around this frame, with the interlocking plastic bricks, in such a way that when holes were made in the walls the interior building acted as a support. Once a prisoner managed to escape he joined the builders and another took his place. This was very cooperative play; the children outside waiting quietly and patiently while the prisoner engineered his escape which they did not try to prevent. When John was in prison he stood for a considerable time making no attempt to escape and looked a little scared and bewildered. Susan went in and showed him a way to climb out, following after herself.

After they had finished their construction play this group of children all spontaneously sat at a table and drew big intricate pencil pictures about Colditz, prisons and escapes. They described the escape routes carefully to each other and to the teacher. She subsequently discussed different kinds of prisons with these children, looking at pictures of castles, prisons and a variety of buildings. Although the boys originally involved always formed the main group, other children joined in. The play continued for several weeks while the television series was being shown.

Teachers can now:

1 analyse the motivation, learning and development in this play
2 answer the question 'How did the teacher structure this play?'

Our analysis and answers can be found in Appendix 1.

Other extensions of the play that might have followed with the help of an adult
1 Expedition to a castle or prison.
2 Erecting a scale model of a castle or a model based on a picture.
3 Making a collection of pictures of castles and forts.
4 Reading and hearing stories about castles and forts and famous escapes.
5 Making up stories of escapes either on tape or in writing.

Other kinds of play based on the same stimulus
Another TV series that is popular in the children's play is *Dr Who*. In several schools children have been observed constructing Daleks from large boxes, barrels, tubs, tubes and rolls of newspaper or cardboard; sometimes they were propelled by the children, sometimes they were static and sometimes the children were able to walk inside

them. In a vertically grouped school, children of different age groups combined to construct a time machine that was large enough for two children to play in, and which had dials and controls made from discarded electrical equipment.

Another frequently observed influence is that of 'wild west' films. Children have made Indian canoes large enough to hold two or three children at a time from cardboard boxes, newspapers and Marvin.

The time machine and the Indian construction both led to frequent reference to books, pictures, diagrams and to adult involvement.

Using Construction Play
1 Provide in turn for the four kinds of stimuli described in construction play.
2 Notice what other stimuli there are in the construction play in your classroom.
3 Notice whether the stimuli under 1 and 2 above motivate the other categories of play.
4 Observe the construction play as often as possible with the intention of participating, where appropriate.
5 Record your objectives for becoming involved.
6 Record the learning and development in the play.

Reference
BURTON, V. (1968) *The Little House* Faber

6 Make/Believe Play

Introduction

In this chapter the teacher's involvement is elaborated. The last description of play is left for teachers to analyse and to answer the question 'How did the teacher structure?' Our analysis and answers are given in Appendix 1.

As explained earlier, the term Make/Believe Play has been used in the Project to cover play with paint, crayons, scrap, collage and dressing-up materials, that involves the children in making and pretending.

Teachers who observed this play recorded many examples of children imagining a situation as they drew or created, or making 'props' to use in their imaginative play: as they draw or paint a picture, they make believe that the aeroplane has shot the parachutist down into the sea and that the ship will rescue him; as they play at being pirates they make black patches and skull and crossbone hats.

Children play with paint, crayons, charcoal, chalk, pencils, glue, paper, cardboard, collage and waste materials. In this way they discover what the materials feel, smell, look and sound like, what can be done with them and how far they can be controlled. Many art and craft books describe the necessity of providing the widest variety of materials possible, and examine the value of allowing children to discover their properties. Before they come to school, children have often been taught to think there is only one way of using tools and materials. Infant teachers do their best to counteract the inhibitions this sometimes causes by providing opportunities for experiments such as finger, hand and foot painting, paper tearing, paint flicking and blow painting. They are careful to word their questions to the children so that they do not think a picture or 'scrap construction' must always be representational. Although they know children need to be shown skills and the safe, correct use of tools, they value willingness to improvise and experiment.

All the art activities of children are not necessarily imaginative and all the make-believe play they engage in does not necessarily require props. In infant schools, make/believe play takes place with sand, water, clay, bricks, dressing-up clothes, on climbing frames and apparatus, in corridors, in outside play areas, with bicycles, cars and large toys. Thus children often play imaginatively without making props. But often they make props for their make/believe play, and conversely the making of props stimulates the play.

Teacher involvement

Some teachers are hesitant about becoming involved in children's imaginative play. They maintain that this is the children's 'secret world' which is necessary as a retreat from the interference of adults. They also argue that adults cannot help but alter the imaginary situation and that their involvement inhibits rather than promotes the children's imagination. They believe that although children copy each other in their make/believe play, the pressure to copy the adult is much greater and the children are more likely to accept the adult's example and suggestions as invariably superior to their own. This point of view must be respected. Children must be free to develop their make/believe play as their own imagination directs them. But some children have not been encouraged in make/believe play before they come to school. Their parents have not had the time or may not have known how to play make/believe with them. They may have had no older children in the family to copy. These children often treat dressing-up clothes roughly, put them on and rush about excitedly. They require careful guidance if they are to enjoy make/believe play. Teachers need to do more for them than just stimulate with stories and poetry or leave them to follow the other children. They may need to initiate the play and provide the original idea for the children to develop as well as joining in and reviving interest with new suggestions and materials. Even highly imaginative children who initiate their own play appreciate the involvement and the ideas of teachers whom they know enjoy and value this play. If adults are involved they should try to:

1 be in sympathy with, understand and value children's make/believe play
2 observe the play first
3 take their cues from the children
4 make provision and suggestions in such a way that the children can easily ignore them
5 be prepared to accept rejection
6 know the purpose of their involvement
7 ensure that their involvement does not make the children dependent on adults for the play.

Materials for make/believe

Teachers are most ingenious in their provision of make/believe materials. They know that varieties of texture, shape and colour lead to imaginative constructions and play. They also know that too much variety at first may confuse the children and lead to extravagance and lack of appreciation of the materials. For this reason they introduce

86

different colours, shapes and textures gradually and store them by categories. At the end of every play session the junk materials are sorted and stored according to texture, shape or colour. By the time the children have been gradually introduced to the full range of materials they know what is available. They know where the materials are kept, how they can be used and how to improvise with them. Even with such experienced children, if a teacher thinks the materials are becoming too familiar, she may suggest that they limit their choice on certain occasions to a restricted range of colours or textures or shapes. In this way she maintains or revives interest and restructures the play.

In the same way that children can be overwhelmed by a profusion of art and junk materials when they are first introduced to them, so they can be confused by a plethora of dressing-up materials. A careful selection that can be reviewed and changed throughout the year is more likely to promote make-believe play than a haphazard collection of clothes which children have to delve into to find something suited to their purpose. This smaller selection, matched to the children's current interests, helps solve the vexed problem of storing dressing-up materials. Children can help the teacher to decide when a new selection needs to be made and what it should comprise.

When all the clothes are not in use at the same time, it is possible to wash, iron and mend them and always to have a fresh supply available. A selection of clean, attractive and easily accessible dressing-up materials is more likely to promote lively make-believe play than a box of dusty, musty, crumpled garments.

The 'all purpose garment'

The essence of make/believe materials is that they should be adaptable and non-prescriptive. Many teachers have experimented to produce 'all purpose garments'. They have made a shapeless robe that can be readily adapted to suit innumerable roles. A variety of coloured felt or material shapes are provided to be stuck on with Velcro so that the children can decorate their robe at will. Alternatively teachers have attached Velcro to lengths of material so that the children can wrap them around each other and suit them to many purposes. Different ways of fastening dressing-up clothes give valuable practice in manipulative skill, but care should be taken to ensure that the fasteners are unbroken and within the children's capability.

Teachers on the Project recorded the popularity of peaked or tall hats that could be worn to represent many roles; of old curtains and lengths of material that could be draped to make many different garments; of cloaks that could be used as skirts and flowing head-dresses.

Cardboard boxes can be 'all purpose' as well. At first a box can become a Dalek; later the same morning, used by another child – or even the same child – it is transformed into a petrol pump on a service station. The 'all purpose' cardboard box and the 'all purpose' dressing-up garment give rise to true make/believe play. They have the added advantage of being easy to provide, easy to replace and comparatively cheap.

Storage

Make/believe materials often cause special storage problems for teachers. Where space is at a premium and it is impossible to find room for a clothes rack, teachers fix a home-made 'tree' in a tub and hang the clothes on the branches or fix clothes hangers on a collapsible 'maiden'. This ensures that the children can quickly see what is available. When not in use the clothes are folded and stored in a cardboard box in the classroom storage cupboard or stockroom.

Art and craft materials are stored in many different ways according to the space available. Some teachers use drawers in the children's storage units and label or identify them with pictures. Others prefer metal trays stored either on a stand or on shelves available to the children. Some of the questions raised about the storage of containers for play with natural materials will apply to the storage of junk materials. Large wire trolleys with two or three compartments are provided in other schools. If there is no sink in the room and the cloakroom is not within easy access, it is often useful to have a large jug or bucket of clean water for each session. Paste brushes can then be washed and returned to their storage place, and not left about after use where they spoil new materials or become hard and difficult to clean. If children are expected to up-end them in a container in between use, they do not spoil their models or collages by being left around on tables or benches. Method and training of this kind is a form of structure that is indispensable to satisfying make/believe play.

Types of materials

The materials that are used for make/believe play are innumerable. Teachers as well as children are inventive and imaginative in the uses they find for materials. We list some that the Project teachers found to be reasonably easy to obtain:

Adhesives: P.V.A., Marvin, Gloy, cold water paste, Copydex,

Sellotape, gummed brown paper roll.

Aprons: plastic, old shirts.

Brushes: paint brushes – all sizes including wallpaper size and toothbrushes, sponges, foam rubber, paste spreaders.

Cardboard: various thicknesses and colours, corrugated.

Charcoal, chalk, felt-tip pens, Magimarkers.

Containers: for glue, possibly yoghurt pots.

Crayons: wax, different thicknesses, pencil type.

Dressing-up materials: lengths of material and net, all purpose garments, cloaks, aprons, hats, shoes.

A mirror, if possible full length and fastened to a wall or cupboard back.

A shelf, rack or bag container for shoes.

A board with hooks on which to hang hats or wigs, loops inside hats for hanging may be useful.

One teacher made a set of hat stands from dowelling, using the children's small building bricks as bases. These are displayed on a shelf and stored away in a cupboard when not in use. Some teachers prefer not to have hats for dressing up; others observe that hats are their children's most popular choice.

Junk materials: boxes, tubes, polystyrene trays and packing, egg boxes, tiles – complete and broken, milk bottle tops, foil containers, ribbon, wood, string, rope, straw and wood shavings, sawdust, straws – plastic and paper, lollipop sticks, wooden spills, wood offcuts, metal offcuts if safe, feathers, cotton-wool, beads, buttons, sequins, carpet scraps, fabric scraps – fraying and non-fraying, Lurex, leather, suede, fur, shells, natural materials – cones, conkers, etc., pencil and old crayon shavings, pasta, netting bags, old curtain rings, corks, doilies – gold, silver, white.

Knives: palette, blunt tableknives.

Modelling materials: flour and salt dough, Play Doh, papier mâché, Plasticine, Polyfilla.

Modelling tools: sticks – all shapes and patterns, sponges, card combs, old waffle iron.

Paint: various kinds – ready-mixed and dry.

Paint containers: these need weekly washes – the children's task.

Paper: kitchen, sugar, duplicating, computer, wallpaper, tissue sheets, circles, squares, gummed paper, matt, shiny, foil – plain and patterned, cellophane sheets and offcuts, magazines,

mail order catalogues, cards – birthday and Christmas, newspapers.
Pencils: various thicknesses.
Scissors: large as well as small – all effective, keyhole or pad saw
for cutting cardboard.

Art play

A teacher had put out on a bench, paper, paint in trays and a collection
of different shaped bricks and cotton reels. She suggested to a group
of five year olds that they could make patterns with the cotton reels
and small bricks. During the morning several children came to the
table and tried out the materials making patterns and alternating
the bricks and reels. Susan however only used the cotton reels and
one colour of paint. First she made one print with each different
patterned reel. Then she took one reel and using the edge drew a house
shape on a fresh sheet of paper. She sorted through the reels and,
selecting one with a thinner edge, drew in the windows and door.
The chimney was made by rolling a cotton reel; this was not successful so she filled in the space with her finger after dipping it in paint.
Susan looked at the paint-covered finger and the following conversation took place with her neighbour.

Susan: Look the paint makes a pattern on my finger.
John: Put it on the paper – don't move it – just press it on.
Susan: It makes a pattern here – it's got like lines on.
John: I've made one – mine doesn't show, it's no good.
Susan: You have to put a lot of paint on – I'll show you – watch me –
        I'm going to do it with my thumb now.
John: I'm painting a picture with my finger. Look you can make
        a picture with your finger – you don't want a brush.
Susan: I made a picture with the cotton reel – you can paint with
        them if you want.

The art and craft specialists have examined and written about the
value of this play from the artist's point of view. They have made us
conscious of how children become aware of colour, pattern, line,
materials and tools. Teachers' recordings also show how children
learn about shape, space, size, conservation, relationships, balance,
angles, symmetry, measurement and weight when they are drawing,
painting, constructing and modelling. Words have meaning when
children use or meet them in a practical situation. Language becomes

necessary when one needs to describe an exciting experience. Sometimes it is easier to talk if one's hands are engaged or one is sharing pleasure in a creative activity.

Problems arise and have to be solved. In this kind of play children are faced with the need to reason, something happens and they want to know why – 'that spot was blue, now it's green, now it's purple'; they want to make something happen and they have to find out how. Manipulative skill and hand and eye coordination are obvious outcomes. Perseverance and concentration frequently occur. Children quick to appreciate the results that ensue when others apply themselves are often encouraged to expend effort in a way that may not come easily to them.

The therapeutic value of this play has been examined many times by educational psychologists and psychiatrists. In their reports teachers sometimes refer to their knowledge of children's backgrounds when they account for the children's play with art materials. It is clear that infant teachers acknowledge the value of 'art play' for children's emotional development.

A skilled teacher observes carefully and evaluates what a child is doing before she decides whether to intervene. Six year old Marie was painting a blue house; as she painted the first window red, the paint trickled down the page. She watched it and then carefully put drops of red, green and yellow paint on top of the blue line of the roof, so that she had trickles of different colours running down her picture. This was a very skilled task although the finished result looked as though it had been haphazard. The normal reaction of a teacher on seeing drips of paint on the painting of a six year old who was expected not to overload her brush, would have been to say, 'Be careful, you are letting the paint drip, wipe your brush first.' Fortunately Marie's teacher had been observing and knew that the experiment had enabled Marie to discover what was the result of mixing blue with other colours. When Marie saw the teacher's interest she said, 'Look, the top line is blue but all the trickles are different colours. They all *come* from the blue.' An adult cannot always be observing when paintings are done but she can know better than to judge by saying, 'What a pity you let the paint run, next time you'll have to wipe your brush, won't you?'

Teachers play with materials to discover their properties, and share in the children's play to give children the chance to see what a more skilled person can do. Some teachers who hesitate to tell a child what to do when he is making a scrap construction, a collage or a picture, may prefer to paint, draw, model or construct alongside him.

They will not suggest that he copy, but know that by watching he learns how to use tools and materials. He may also be prompted to ask questions and seek advice. For example, another child might have been experimenting like Marie and prevented from making a discovery by a well-intentioned teacher's intervention; whereas if the child had been able to watch and discover how to prevent the paint dripping there would have been no possibility of misdirected intervention by an adult. The adult playing alongside children can be demonstrating a skill and encouraging them to try their own experiments or use their imagination at the same time. Many children never see adults drawing, painting, or devising scrap constructions; even the teacher only admires theirs, and never apparently makes her own. We all comment on the need for children to see adults enjoying and profiting from reading. We all know how appreciative children are if we tell them we made or drew something. Yet we seldom let them see us at these ploys.

Make/believe stories

When children are drawing, painting or making models from collage and scrap materials they make up situations or stories as they play. Sometimes they use the materials to illustrate their story and sometimes the materials themselves seem to stimulate their imagination.

I   THE LORRY

Two five year olds, Frances and Simon, were crayonning. Frances drew a cat and Simon a lorry. When Frances asked Simon what was in his lorry, he told her 'Weetabix', and began drawing the boxes. He explained to Frances that the lorry was going to a supermarket, whereupon she said she would draw the supermarket on another piece of paper.

Simon then pretended to drive the lorry to the shop, and Frances drew the Weetabix boxes in the shop window. Simon next pretended to be the lorry driver getting the boxes off the lorry. They decided the lorry would go better if it was cut out; this prompted them to cut the doors of the supermarket so that they would open.

Frances: What have you got in the back of your lorry?
Simon: I'm taking a load of Weetabix to the supermarket.
Frances: I will draw a supermarket with big fat doors so that you can get your lorry in.
Simon: Don't be silly, the lorry doesn't go inside the supermarket.

> The driver unloads the lorry by the doors. He has to reverse it up to the doors.

Frances: The window must be as big as the classroom ones to get all the Weetabix in it.

Simon: Oh dear! The man can't get out of the lorry because he hasn't got a door. (Draws the door and handle.) Now he can get out. Knock! Knock! Is the supermarket open yet?

Frances: I can't write supermarket. I'll ask Mrs S how to spell it.

Simon: I'll go and get in my cab and have a sleep while you write supermarket on your shop.

At this point Mrs S was asked to write 'supermarket' for them and Frances copied it on top of the drawing of her shop. Then Simon pretended to wake up and said, 'Now I will open up the supermarket. Oh! I'd better cut the door open then I can get in.' He took the scissors, opened the doorway, and at that point decided to cut out his lorry too so that he could back it up to the doors. He asked Mrs S to help him with the wheels because it wouldn't go properly if they were not round. Simon then asked if she would draw a warehouse because he wanted to bring his lorry back to it. He explained that he needed to get some lollipops and chocolate to put into the supermarket window as the Weetabix would not fill it up. Mrs S drew a warehouse and Simon returned with the lorry. Lollipops and chocolate were now drawn on the back of the lorry on top of the original Weetabix boxes which were ignored. When the children copied the word 'supermarket' and watched the teacher write 'warehouse' they commented that 'supermarket' was a bigger word than 'warehouse' although they were both big words. They then counted the letters in each and were surprised the difference was so small. When Frances drew the Weetabix boxes in the window, they both counted to see if she had got as many as the lorry had brought. Mrs S suggested to Simon that the lorry needed a name. Simon said, 'Don't be silly! A lorry doesn't have a name.' It was suggested that some lorries had owners' names on them. Simon said that his hadn't, but Frances said she had seen names on lorries and Simon ought to look on lorries and see them himself. Simon looked out for lorries with names on when he went home. The following day the teacher asked Simon if he had looked at the lorries; he said he had seen some lorries with names on, but he had also seen a lot without names on them. (This was obviously to justify the fact that he hadn't put a name on the drawing of his own lorry.)

The make/believe situation had been much more real to Simon than Frances and he had enjoyed being the lorry driver. He must have observed a lorry reversing because he really made the most of that part and accompanied his play with appropriate noises.

Examples of motivation, learning and development that occurred in this play

1 Frances was inspired to join in Simon's play when he explained what he was imagining.
2 The children practised their use of language; they reasoned, reported, imagined, projected.
3 They counted and matched the number of Weetabix boxes and compared the numbers of letters in two words.
4 They estimated the size of doors and windows for their drawings.
5 They reasoned about the shape of the wheels and the necessity for round wheels.
6 Manipulative skills were practised in drawing, cutting and writing.
7 The children were motivated to read and write.
8 Simon was motivated to observe accurately.
9 Concentration was maintained for forty minutes.
10 Interest was sustained out of school hours and until the following day.

HOW DID THE TEACHER STRUCTURE THIS PLAY?

1 By providing the materials for crayonning and encouraging the children to combine materials.
2 By involvement.

How did the teacher become involved?

1 She was asked by the children to write 'supermarket' and 'warehouse' on the drawings.
2 She was asked to help with the wheels of the lorry.
3 She was asked to draw a warehouse and told by the children to make big doors and to cut them so that they opened ready for the lorry.
4 By suggesting that lorries have names.

Why did the teacher become involved?

1 Because the children wished her to participate in their play.
2 Because she did not wish them to abandon their play when they set themselves a task beyond their capabilities, e.g. when Simon

could not cut out a circle, she gave the minimum of assistance and left him to cut out the remainder of the lorry.

3 Because she wanted to encourage the children in their request to incorporate reading and writing in their play.

What was the result of the teacher's involvement?

1 The children incorporated reading and writing in their play.
2 They compared the words she wrote and counted the letters.
3 Simon was motivated to observe lorries carefully.
4 The children had to explain clearly what was happening in their play.
5 They realized that Mrs S valued this play and was interested.

2 THE ZOO

Jacqueline and Serena, both six year olds, said they wanted to make a picture about the zoo, so their teacher gave them a large piece of paper and they knelt on the floor with their crayons. They started to draw the animals in the zoo, and the coach coming to the entrance; gradually a story took shape.

Jacqueline:	This little girl and her mummy have got off the coach and now they're going to the entrance. They're paying their money.
Serena:	Here's the elephant – he's giving rides to the children.
Jacqueline:	It's the sea lions' pool – the keeper's giving them their dinner – this one's just catching a fish. His brother's swimming up for one too.
Serena:	This is where the monkeys are – they're climbing all over.
Jacqueline:	One's escaped he's jumped over here – he's running along this path, he's near the sea lions' pool now. He's frightened. He doesn't know where to go. All the people are shouting.
Serena:	The little girl's seen him – she's put him in her bag – he's only a little monkey.
Jacqueline:	Her mummy doesn't know – she's looking at the parrots. Here's an ant she's treading on it.
Serena:	This is a little mouse – he's the monkey's friend – he's climbing up in the bag to keep him company.
Jacqueline:	They're going home now, the coach is coming back for them. The driver's had his tea. He's honking his horn.
Serena:	No he's not, 'cos they know which is their coach. The little girl's taking the monkey and the mouse home.

Their teacher had overheard the end of the story and asked the girls if they would like her to help them to write it down so that they could read it to the other children. They agreed and later showed their illustration to a group as they read the story. The next day they asked if they could make a book and together with their teacher worked out how many illustrations they could make and which sections of the writing should go alongside. This book was left in the library for the other children to enjoy.

Examples of motivation, learning and development that occurred in this play

1 The two girls cooperated in drawing, in telling the story to the other children and in writing their book.
2 They resolved their disagreements about the selection of illustrations to match the writing in their story book.
3 They used language in different ways when they made up their story: they reasoned, reported, imagined, projected.
4 They measured accurately when cutting the pages and stapling them together for their book. They also numbered the pages.
5 They solved the problem caused when one of their illustrations was too small for the page. They drew a border of all the animals in their zoo.
6 They had to manoeuvre in order not to obstruct each other when they drew their original picture.
7 Manipulative skill was required for drawing, writing and stapling the book.
8 Interest in the story motivated them to describe their picture, write a book and finally read the story aloud to a large group of children.
9 Other children in the class were motivated to read the book in the class library.
10 Other children in the class were motivated to write and illustrate books for the class library.
11 Serena and Jacqueline concentrated for periods of from twenty minutes to an hour. Their interest was sustained over three days.
12 They were concerned that their book should be aesthetically pleasing and repeatedly asked the teacher's opinion about choice of colour and placing their illustrations.

HOW DID THE TEACHER STRUCTURE THIS PLAY?

1 By providing:
    (a) paper large enough for two children to draw on

(b) writing materials for the girls to make a book about their picture story

(c) a class library that included books made and written by the children.

2   By involvement.

How did the teacher become involved?

1   The girls told her that they wanted to make a zoo picture. She gave them the materials, the space to work together and sufficient time to complete their drawing.

2   She observed their play and realized that they were inventing a story as they drew.

3   She suggested they should write the story and offered to help.

4   She showed them how to sort out the sequence of illustrations for their book to match the illustrations to the text.

Why did the teacher become involved?

1   She wanted to encourage the girls to cooperate in their play.

2   Jacqueline was normally unwilling to write. The teacher used the incentive of her drawing and cooperation with Serena as motivation.

3   The teacher wanted to revive the interest of other children in making books for the library.

What was the result of the teacher's involvement?

1   The two girls encouraged each other; jointly they were able to suggest sufficient incidents and develop a sequence that made a complete story.

2   The children recorded their story.

3   Other children heard the story and looked at the original picture. They were motivated to make up their own picture stories.

4   Jacqueline and Serena divided their story into sections with appropriate illustrations. This was a difficult process for them requiring thought about the sequence of events and the content of the illustrations. It gave rise to much discussion and decision making. The teacher's advice was often sought at the beginning but after the first three illustrations the girls became more self-reliant.

Cowboys and Indians

In a vertically grouped class a group of children often played Cowboys and Indians using the Wendy house as a wigwam or camp. This frequently caused arguments with the children who were engaged in domestic play.

The teacher asked the children why they didn't make a wigwam for their play.

'We don't know how,' was the chorus.

'Go and find all the books you can in the library with pictures of Indians and their camps and we'll see what they look like and work out how they are made,' suggested the teacher.

This was Miss B's usual approach and the children knew their way about the library. Later they examined the pictures and had a lively discussion about totem poles, wigwams, Indian designs, moccasins, bead patterns and head-dresses. As it was home time they arranged that they would bring from home anything they thought they could use and that could be spared to make Indian clothes, a wigwam and a totem pole.

Before school the next morning, Miss B put a length of sacking and some canes with the collage materials and paint. The children came into school with their offerings; large tubes, cardboard boxes of all sizes and shapes, collections of beads, and feathers and some old sheeting. They seized the canes and sacking and without prompting decided, 'it's just right for our wigwam'. This group of children were accustomed to organizing themselves when they were making collage constructions and pictures. They apportioned the jobs, calling on Miss B for advice and help when they were stuck. During the next few days they made a wigwam, a large totem pole, chief's and braves' head-dresses, axes, bows and arrows, squaws' tunics, belts and pouches. They did not cease their make/believe play during this period. Head-dresses, tunics and belts were added as the play progressed.

The wigwam was reconstructed three times as there were difficulties to overcome in erecting it and making it stable. The totem pole was reassembled and embellished because the children were disappointed that it was not as large and as colourful as they wanted it to be. Frequent reference was made to pictures and books. Miss B read stories about Polutin and taped them so that they could be used with the tape recorder. Many books and pictures were brought from home and a collection of Indian dolls was added to the Indian display that the children arranged in a corridor. The group had wanted to set up their camp in the outside play area but wet weather interfered with their plans. They settled for a corridor and in this way all the school became interested in the play. Some of the children involved wrote and drew descriptions of their play, others made up stories that they read to Miss B and to the others in the group. Many were observed reading books that contained information or tales about Indians. Miss B adapted passages from the story *The Antelope Singer* which contained information about the customs that enabled Indian tribes to survive in severe winters.

Examples of motivation, learning and development that occurred in this play

1   Cooperation was essential in most of this play. Children needed to help each other in the making, and the make/believe situation caused frequent social interaction.

2   Home and school cooperated. Parents sent scrap and display materials and shared their children's enthusiasm and interest.

3   Dialogue fostered language. Children had to explain their difficulties to each other and to adults; to describe what they were doing; to predict and to project: 'If I put this here will the totem pole be too high?' 'Don't put it there, it's straight off the fire – it's hot, it will burn the stool,' 'You're so ill you will have to go to the witch-doctor and get him to make a spell for you.'

4   New vocabulary was acquired, e.g. tomahawk, tepee, moccasin.

5   Children used books, they read story and information books, they pored over pictures. Those who could not read examined pictures in detail. They read and some learnt by heart the notices Miss B and other children made for display and for use in their play.

6   Children wrote and drew about their play. Miss B did not have to instigate this; it was customary in the school for children to write and illustrate their own books. Miss B had always encouraged make/believe play because she had found it provided interest and motivation for writing. Children who were unable to write, drew and told Miss B what they wanted to write so that they could copy her transcript.

7   Much mathematical knowledge was applied, e.g. beads were counted to make patterns; children were measured for tunics and head-dresses and the sizes written down and later made into histograms. (Miss B had put out tape measures but the younger children discovered that a piece of string is easier to use.) Symmetry was understood when patterns were made.

8   Hand and eye coordination and manual dexterity were necessary for making and erecting props and for many of the actions involved in Indian activities.

9 Physical skill was necessary, especially to set up the totem pole and wigwam.

10 Many problems were encountered and most solved. For example, the wigwam supports caused arguments; at first they had three canes but later, after several collapses, four. The sacks were difficult to drape around the canes but were stapled together.

> Jennifer: They look like the animal skins the Indians used – all patchy – my mum's making a patchwork quilt.

There were not enough feathers for head-dresses so they fringed and decorated paper. They discovered paper feathers were 'floppy', so substituted thin card. Hessian tote bags from the dressing-up store were made into papoose slings; a large one was used for twins!

HOW DID THE TEACHER STRUCTURE THIS PLAY?

1 By providing:
   (a) space – she made the corridor space available to extend the play.
   (b) time – she allowed the play to continue as long as the interest was expressed. This was possible because the school followed an integrated programme.
   (c) materials – she brought new materials to extend the play, e.g. canes and sacking. She encouraged the children to bring materials from home.
   (d) fresh stimulus at intervals by introducing new stories, books and pictures, and facilitating the display of Indian dolls and ornaments. Information the children required was already available in a form they could understand: in this case books at their reading level in the school library.
2 By involvement.

How did the teacher become involved?

1 Miss B intervened because she had been observing the play and judged that an adult's intervention was required in order to settle the children's argument about the use of the Wendy house.
2 She encouraged the children to improvise so that in future make/believe play they would not be frustrated by lack of props.
3 She was ready to advise and help when the children sought her aid but otherwise left them to organize themselves and make their own decisions.
4 She showed the children new skills.

5 She discussed the play with the children.
6 She showed interest and gave encouragement throughout the play.

Why did the teacher become involved?
1 Because she was concerned that the Indian play clashed with the domestic play and it became obvious that the children were not able to resolve their claims to the house without her assistance.
2 Because her observation of the Indian play revealed that the children were repeating the same sequence over and over again. She decided that they needed some fresh stimulus to promote the imaginary situation which obviously held their interest.
3 Because she knew that there were several books about Indians in the school library that could be used. She wanted to encourage two boys in particular in the group to value books. They were unwilling readers and she intended through the interest in Indians to help them to persevere.
4 Because she saw the opportunity to enter into discussion with the children and, by talking about Indians, foster their language development.
5 Because the children had frequently made large constructions with cardboard boxes and other scrap material. They had experience of making patterns in many different ways. Miss B knew that they could utilize these skills to promote and extend their make/believe play. She hoped that they and other children would realize that they could also make props for different make/believe situations.
6 Because she wanted to give this group of children the opportunity to organize their 'making' play. Previously groups had been of two, three or four children, not eight as this time.
7 Because it was obvious that many problems would arise in the 'prop' making, Miss B wanted to create a situation where the children's interest would sustain them through problem solving and reasoning. If she had assessed their involvement in this make/believe play correctly she believed it would motivate them to persevere, to apply knowledge and skills already gained and acquire new ones.
8 Because she wished to help the group to realize that 'fighting' play could become more than pretend physical aggression, because her observations led her to think that the children were soon bored with the 'fighting', and that the play and the group disintegrated after the first few minutes. Also boisterous 'fighting' play interfered with other children's activities.

What was the result of the teacher's involvement?

1   The domestic play could continue without interruptions.

2   The other class activities were no longer disrupted by the haphazard fighting of Indians.

3   The Indian group became aware of Miss B's interest and that she valued their play.

4   The interest in this play was sustained for several weeks and a group of children therefore cooperated throughout this time.

5   The group had practice in organizing their play; they had to make decisions, give orders to, and accept orders from, their peers.

6   The make/believe play situation was developed, e.g. they played Indian village life and ceremonies.

7   The children's role play was extended; they became squaws, braves, chiefs and papooses.

8   There was the need for much dialogue; vocabulary was increased and language fostered.

9   Mathematical knowledge had to be applied and consolidated.

10 Books were read and pictures observed in detail.

11 Children and teachers were encouraged to watch 'western' films carefully. It was hoped that this might foster careful observation in other situations.

12 Children wrote stories and made illustrated books about different aspects of their Indian make/believe.

13 Perseverance and concentration were applied to the play.

14 She did not need to forbid fighting and cause dissension between herself and the group engaged in noisy and energetic play. She harnessed their interest and showed them how to further it in ways that achieved her educational objectives and was much more satisfying to them.

A play situation in many ways similar to this Indian play involved a group of six and seven year olds. They were reading a series of reading books about pirates. When they started to be pirates in their play and to steal and bury gold their teacher asked them if they would like to make the treasure and pirates' clothes. Over several weeks one area of the room was transformed into a pirates' cave; clothes and properties were made and as more make-believe situations were developed more materials and props were devised and constructed. The teacher fostered the play because this group of children had lost interest in reading which they found boring. She wanted to encourage them to refer to books, enjoy reading and see that it had purpose.

As in the Indian play the children counted, measured, developed an understanding of space, size and shape, drew buried treasure maps, talked a great deal, wrote notices, captions and stories, consulted books and pictures.

Witches

Often imaginative play may involve one or two children only and a teacher may question whether she is justified in spending the time to develop the play of one or two children. Criteria she might consider are:

1 whether her suggestions could be related to other situations by different groups of children who are aware of what is happening
2 whether the one or two children concerned could transfer the ideas of the new play situations and involve more children in the future
3 whether the learning and development that result for one or two children merit the time given
4 whether the motivation, for example to read or write, that will result from the play is important. Are these children who are seldom motivated?

An example of this type of play was recorded by Mrs E.

Two six year olds, Jennifer and Timothy, were playing together on a carpeted area. Jennifer was wearing a cloak and Timothy had a foxfur tail tied on his back. They had brought some cooking utensils from the domestic play corner and arranged them around a stool. Jennifer was stirring in a saucepan on the stool and Timothy was crawling along the carpet.

Jennifer: Where is the cat? He's never here when I want him. Cat, where are you?
Timothy: I'm here – I'm in the wood.
Jennifer: Well, I'm making the dinner, it'll be ready in a minute. I'm doing a spell. I know I'll go in the garden and get some poison.
Timothy: I don't like poison.
Jennifer: Yes, you do. Witches and their cats all like poison. They always eat poison for their dinners. Now what other ingredients shall I put in. (She looked up and saw Mrs E watching.) Are you coming to dinner? Would you like to be a visitor? This is the witch's house.

Mrs E:	I don't know, I've never been to dinner with a witch. Do they have guests to dinner?
Jennifer:	Oh yes, they like having visitors come in – here's a seat for you.
Mrs E:	What are we having for dinner? I'm very particular about what I eat.
Jennifer:	I'm making a stew – it's got poison in.
Mrs E:	Oh, then I don't think I'll stay – I'll die if I eat poison, I'm not a witch, nor a witch's cat.
Jennifer:	Oh, it's all right. I don't give visitors poison. I'm making something special for you – just a minute, I'll look it up in the book – this is a proper cook book you see. Cat, go and get me some proper food from the shop.
Timothy:	All right, give me the money.
Jennifer:	Witches don't have money. You'll have to magic it from the shop.
Timothy:	All right – goodbye . . . Here I am back now, here's the stuff.
Jennifer:	Thank you – now I'll cook your dinner. Carrots and onions and meat. What would you like for afters? (She put shells, conkers and buttons in the pot.)
Mrs E:	Please don't give me too much, I only have a little appetite.
Jennifer:	Are you slimming? Witches don't have diets – I can eat everything. This is mine – I'll give you a littler one. Here you are cat, here's yours. Eat it all up quickly 'cos you've got a lot of work to do.
Mrs E:	Thank you very much, I must go now. Would you like another cook book with new recipes in? What kind of ingredients did you get from the garden?
Jennifer:	Oh – herbs and things. I wish I had a witch's cook book.
Mrs E:	Well, goodbye cat, goodbye witch, thank you for my dinner.

Mrs E left and Jennifer washed up and went out on her broomstick with her cat.

Later in the morning Mrs E reminded Jennifer and Timothy of their play. She asked Jennifer if she would like to write a recipe book for a witch, and Timothy what the cat's name was. Jennifer started to make the cover of her book. Timothy said he didn't have a name but he didn't like to be called just 'cat'. He then painted a large picture of a cat. Mrs E wrote under Timothy's cat, 'Please give this witch's cat a name' and displayed it alongside Jennifer's book cover 'The Witch Cook Book'. She added a notice to the cover saying, 'Please put your recipes in the witch's sack'. When other children began to be interested the next morning, Mrs E gathered a group together with Jennifer and Timothy and discussed cats' names and witches' recipes. There was a collection of stories and books about cats for them to look at and Mrs E discussed herbs and weeds and measures: two pinches of, an acorncup full. Other ingredients such as dead frogs, black beetles, spiders and worms were all suggested. Then they thought about shaking, stirring and mixing. Finally Mrs E left the children who wanted to write out their recipes using the list of words she had made during the discussion; she offered to spell out any others that were needed. Timothy and a few others looked at the cat stories and during the day several children put names in the bag. Before home time Timothy chose his name from those submitted: Arthur!

Later in the week, Mrs E observed many games of witches and that the recipe book was used, read and caused much amusement. She was pleased that she had been invited to join in the play for two reasons:

1 Jennifer was not accustomed to spend much time reading and writing although she was very talkative. Mrs E took the opportunity to show her how she could use writing in her play.
2 Timothy was a very shy and inarticulate child. She wanted to encourage his involvement with other children and to foster his language. He was not embarrassed by the leading part he took in the cat naming because it had arisen easily from his play and painting.

Note: Jennifer used the word 'ingredients' and yet said 'littler'. Many examples of children employing 'difficult' words while still making grammatical errors are recorded by teachers observing play.

Examples of motivation, learning and development that occurred in this play
1 Timothy gained confidence from being involved in play with Jennifer and Mrs E. Also he enjoyed the attention he received from the naming of his cat picture.
2 Jennifer and Timothy cooperated in the play. Jennifer had the dominant role but Timothy tried to assert his position, e.g. 'I don't like poison', 'give me the money', 'I'm in the wood'.

3 Language was used for reasoning, reporting, imagining, directing, self-maintenance and predicting.
4 New vocabulary was acquired: recipe, witches' brew, bewitch, eerie, cauldron.
5 Problems were solved.
6 Manipulative skill was practised in the pretend cooking and the dressing-up.
7 Concentration was necessary to sustain and follow up the play with drawing, reading and writing.
8 Motivation to discuss, paint, read and write resulted.

HOW DID THE TEACHER STRUCTURE THIS PLAY?
1 By providing:
   (a) adaptable dressing-up materials that gave rise to imaginative play
   (b) space for the play to develop inside and outside the witch's house
   (c) time for the extension of the play in painting and writing
   (d) the materials for making the recipe book
   (e) books about witches and cats in the class library.
2 By involvement.

How did the teacher become involved?
1 By observing the play.
2 By Jennifer's invitation to dinner.
3 By participating in the play and initiating the discussion about recipes and recipe books.

Why did the teacher become involved?
1 Because her observation revealed the possibilities for developing the play.
2 Because she saw the opportunity in the play to motivate Jennifer to read and write.
3 Because she thought she could develop the play situation to promote Timothy's self-confidence and language.

What was the result of the teacher's involvement?
1 Jennifer was able to sustain her dialogue about the meal, to include recipes and slimming.
2 Timothy gained in confidence and began to establish his position in the class.
3 More children became interested in the play. Mrs E hoped there

would be some transfer of imaginative ideas and reading and writing to other play situations.

4 The children realized that their teacher valued make/believe play.
5 The motivation to read and write was provided for many children.
6 Discussions were promoted.
7 Interest was maintained in the imaginative ideas of the play.

Puppet show

Several children in a class of six year olds (the oldest class in this infant school) had been interested in making puppets from scrap materials. They used different shaped cardboard boxes and different sized tins and boxes with buttons, corks, wool, material and bottle tops for decoration. After they had played with the puppets on a bench and table for several days they decided to make a Punch and Judy show. Different kinds of puppet theatres they had seen on television were discussed with the teacher. The headmistress, Mrs M, collected together all the books she could find with pictures of puppets and puppet theatres. Eventually three children, one girl and two boys, started to make the theatre. Peter was the leader of the group. He arrived one morning with his mother carrying a large cardboard box that his father had begged from a local store. It was the container for a washing machine. Many children are content to leave the box unpainted but this group wanted to paint the box. They said all puppet theatres were brightly coloured. Peter, who had been very interested in a Punch and Judy show he had seen on holiday, suggested different coloured stripes. The children started to paint the box but soon stopped when they saw the results.

Rebecca: It won't do – look.
Peter: It don't show the stripes.
Patrick: No, the writing shows through.
Rebecca: The paint's not thick enough.
Peter: The writing's too black, it shows through.
Patrick: Let's ask Miss T if we can make the paint thicker.

Miss T agreed with the children that the painting was not successful but explained to them how expensive paint was. She asked them to think of another way of decorating the box that would not need thicker paint.

Patrick: I know what we can do – put sticky paper on, then we won't use any paint.

Rebecca:	That's no good – sticky paper costs a lot – I know, Mrs R said we hadn't to use too much when we were in her class. 'Sides it's only in small pieces.
Peter:	Let's cover it in newspaper like we did that treasure chest at Christmas. You can paint newspaper.
Patrick:	That's a good idea. Get started.
Rebecca:	We'll have to measure the newspaper first.
Peter:	No, you do it like this – look I'll show you 'cos I helped with the treasure chest. You get the newspaper and hold it up against the box – that's right, now paste that bit on.
Rebecca:	No Patrick – don't put paste all over – just down the sides and a bit in the middle like this.
Peter:	Now fold the bottom over inside – see.
Patrick:	No, it's better to put the bottom of the paper at the bottom of the box like this. Now if this other bit's too long you can fold it over the top. See like this.
Peter:	These pieces of newspaper are smaller, they're better, aren't they?
Rebecca:	Yeah, use them, my dad has that paper.

Miss T left the children to solve the problem of covering the box and by the end of the morning it was complete. As they went to lunch she joined in their conversation.

Peter:	It'll be dry enough when we come back – we can paint it this afternoon. It took a lot of newspaper didn't it? I bet it took hundreds.
Patrick:	'Course it didn't – not hundreds.
Peter:	I bet there were sixty then.
Miss T:	You can count them when you go back. How many do *you* think you used, Rebecca?
Rebecca:	I don't know – about thirty I should think.
Patrick:	Well, I only used four on top.
Miss T:	Well, was the top bigger than the sides? Did it take more sheets of newspaper than each side?

When the children came back in the afternoon, Miss T had an 'estimation chart' for the children to write in their guesses before they counted the sheets of newspaper on the top and the sides. During the afternoon the newspaper was painted and yet another discovery was made and another decision taken.

Peter:	Look it's no good now – the paint's still not thick enough.
Patrick:	Why not? Mine's all right.
Peter:	Well the writing shows through mine.
Rebecca:	It's not writing, it's printing in a newspaper.
Patrick:	It doesn't show through mine.
Rebecca:	It's the dark paint – it doesn't show through the dark paint – the blue and the purple. Yours is yellow Peter.
Patrick:	Let's have blue and purple stripes then.
Rebecca:	Yes, that's what we'll do – just have blue and purple stripes. You two do that side and I'll do this side. We'd better make all the stripes the same size. We don't want fat and thin ones.
Peter:	How'll we know how fat yours are then?
Rebecca:	Do what my mum does when she turns up her dresses – measure with this bit of cardboard.
Patrick:	What do you mean? – I don't know what to do.
Rebecca:	Look all the stripes are going to be as fat as this. Put this piece of cardboard on and make a mark with your brush like I'm doing. Now paint the stripe down from there – see?

By home time the painting was finished and the puppet box was left to dry. The group had decided that they did not want curtains like Peter's seaside Punch and Judy show: 'They didn't have curtains on the tele.'

The next morning the children got their puppets and started to play with them in the theatre.

| Peter: | It's not big enough. We'll have to kneel down so you can't see us only the puppets. |

After a while the children found this very hard on their knees and started to complain.

| Rebecca: | I know let's stand it on the big bricks – those square ones like boxes. |

But the children playing with the bricks were not willing to destroy their building. Miss T suggested the puppeteers fasten the theatre to two smaller boxes which would raise it. They discussed this and voted against it as it would take so long to paint more newspaper and cover more boxes. Miss T then told them to walk round the school to see if they could find something suitable and to ask if they could have it. After a while they returned with a small circular table that was used for displays in the hall. The puppet theatre was lifted on to it and the children's play continued. Mrs M noticed the theatre was unsteady and offered a larger table. As the children played with their puppets, Peter began to make their play into the Punch and Judy story that he remembered from his holiday. The next morning Miss T helped him to work out the story by asking him to tell it to her and the group. Peter went away to write it as a story book. He spent several days illustrating the scenes in the story in between playing with the puppets. There were four characters in the story, which was Peter's own adaptation of the Punch and Judy story. Another boy, Martin, joined the group and made a policeman puppet. When the play was finished, Peter asked if they could do it for the other children. Miss T suggested that they should advertise and make programmes. They looked at two posters advertising a youth club play in a neighbouring comprehensive school and examined some of the programmes. Rebecca painted two posters, one for the classroom door and one for the school entrance hall. The remainder of the group made programmes and tickets. They consulted a seating plan that Miss T brought to show them and lettered and numbered the seats and the tickets. Three children asked if they could sell the tickets before the show started and number the seats in accordance with the plan. Peter was pleased to have their cooperation. Two performances were given on each of two days.

The play only lasted a few minutes but the audience enjoyed buying their tickets and choosing a seat on the plan. The group became adept at explaining the seating arrangement, selling tickets and programmes and counting up the proceeds to tally with the tickets and programmes sold. Miss T provided real money from the shopping play and a bank was set up at the entrance to the classroom. The children from the other classes went to the bank to draw their money to pay for the tickets and the programmes. Two bankers kept accounts of the amount of money they issued and the number of customers. Their accounts were checked at the end with the takings.

Examples of motivation, learning and development that occurred in this play

1 The children cooperated to solve problems and learned from each other.
2 They used language to reason, report, imagine, direct, maintain their position, predict and project. They also developed their

language in reading and writing. They gained confidence from acting in the play.

3 They estimated, counted and measured.
4 They exchanged money.
5 They reinforced their concepts of space, size, shape and time.
6 They acquired and practised manipulative skills.
7 They improved their coordination.
8 They solved many problems.
9 They were inventive in their use of materials.
10 They consulted books and examined pictures, plans, programmes, posters.
11 They wrote and read.
12 They made books which gave pleasure to other children, e.g. Peter also made a diary recording the puppet show. His books were added to the class library.
13 They persevered, concentrated and sustained the play during several days.
14 They experienced the satisfaction of planning and carrying out a project.
15 They transferred knowledge gained in different situations, e.g. from dressmaking.

HOW DID THE TEACHER STRUCTURE THIS PLAY?
1 By providing:
  (a) space for the puppet theatre and audience
  (b) space and equipment for the bank
  (c) materials for the posters, programmes and tickets, real money
  (d) materials for the puppet theatre
  (e) puppets from a variety of materials to arouse the children's interests in puppets and the opportunity to play with puppets
  (f) books about puppets and puppet theatres, stories about puppets.
2 By involvement.

How did the teacher become involved?
1 Before the Punch and Judy show Miss T had been involved in the children's play with puppets in the class:
  (a) She had encouraged the children to make their own puppets from scrap materials and to be inventive in the use of the materials, e.g. noses from bottle tops pressed on to boxes.
  (b) She had played with the puppets *she* made, making up a short repetitive story and encouraging the children to join in.

(c) She had repeated her story several times so that the children became familiar with it and played it when she was not there.

(d) She had helped the children to make up a story about the puppets *they* had made. They were accustomed to help her make up stories in story time – occasionally about a picture or a toy.

(e) She had suggested they make more puppets to suit the characters they had introduced in their story.

(f) When several children made puppets from *The Three Little Pigs*, she had told the story for them as they and their puppets joined in the repetitive chorus. In this way she structured their puppet play, from free play to the point where they were ready to make up their own plays and act them.

2 When the group of children decided to make their puppet theatre for the Punch and Judy show the teacher was involved again:

(a) She discussed puppet theatres with the children.

(b) She examined with them books provided in the school library.

(c) She encouraged them to find materials that would suit their purpose. (If Peter had not brought a box Miss T was ready to offer two she had obtained herself.)

(d) She joined in their discussion about the amount of newspaper used, introduced an estimation chart.

(e) She helped them solve the problem about the height of the theatre.

(f) She suggested that Peter should make a book of his story.

(g) She made a specimen seating plan so that the children could see how to number their tickets and seats.

(h) She arranged that other teachers in the school would co-operate in providing additional audiences.

(i) She brought programmes and posters for the children to study.

(j) She enabled the children to set up a bank.

(k) She encouraged other children to be involved, e.g. the bank clerks she helped.

Why did the teacher become involved?

1 Miss T's observation of the children's interest in making and playing with puppets made her think it could provide the motivation for a cooperative effort.

2 The children obviously wanted to make a Punch and Judy show

and did not know how to make a puppet theatre. They were unable to make a theatre without some guidance.

3 She knew from her previous involvement in puppet play in the class that this group of children were ready to make up their own story.

4 She thought the children were ready to organize their impromptu puppet plays and develop them into a 'show' that involved other children.

5 Her advice was sought about the paint problem.

6 Her advice was sought about raising the theatre.

7 Miss T saw how writing would help Peter to sort out the details of the story.

8 She saw that the other children would be motivated to read Peter's story in order to remember their parts.

9 She could suggest the incorporation of activities that gave practice in mathematics.

10 She could foster the children's language by discussing the play and the show with them.

11 She could help the children to sustain a play situation by suggesting ideas they could adopt if they wished and by introducing new materials.

What was the result of the teacher's involvement?

1 The children developed their ability to play with puppets from rapid play involving repetitive and imitative language to a sustained story.

2 The children were encouraged to improvise in building the theatre and to provide their own materials.

3 They went to consult books about puppet theatres.

4 They learned about the cost of materials and the reason for economy and care in their use.

5 They compared sizes and shapes, e.g. of the top and bottom of the box. This may have been connected with the subsequent wish to make the stripes equal in width.

6 They were encouraged to estimate and count.

7 They were given the opportunity to find their own solutions, e.g. to the problem of raising the theatre.

8 Peter wrote and illustrated his story.

9 The children were shown how to observe posters.

10 They learnt how to read a programme.

11 They used their counting ability to make the seating plan and number seats and tickets.

12 There was motivation to be accurate in using money for programmes and tickets.
13 The suggestion was made that for their next puppet play they could provide a sweet stall or have an ice-cream attendant. They proposed cooking their own refreshments. This resulted from a study of the youth club programmes which offered refreshments at 5p.
14 Other classes in the school were involved in the play.
15 Children in the class were motivated to devise their own puppet plays.

A wedding

A group of five year olds informed their teacher that they were being married and were getting ready for the wedding. She ascertained that there was a bride and groom and two bridesmaids, but was called away and could take no interest in the play that day. When she noticed that it continued the next morning, she found time to talk with the group which had increased to eight because it now included those playing 'house'. As a result of discussion they identified themselves as bride, groom, two bridesmaids, mother, father, best man and the vicar. It transpired that one of the girls had recently acted as bridesmaid at her aunty's wedding; she was very well informed and had obviously taken great interest in the wedding ceremony and its preparations. Bouquets, buttonholes, wedding and bridesmaids' dresses and head-dresses, top hats, and a vicar's surplice were declared necessary. The dresses were selected from the dressing-up rack, but bouquets, buttonholes, head-dresses and a top hat were missing. It was suggested that they could be made; the children collected beads, tissue and coloured paper, cardboard, paint, glue and scissors. The welfare assistant offered to help them, but they said they could manage. After a while her advice was sought; how could they make the stalks for the screwed-up tissue-paper flower heads? They talked about how she made artificial flowers and the way a florist strengthened flowers. She offered to bring some florists' wires the next day. The children did not want to wait so long. 'I know,' said the father, 'straws would do.'

The next problem was the top hat. 'How do you put the tops and bottom on – we've made the middle with this cardboard?' Here the adult could help, she demonstrated the use of brown gummed paper strips cut off a large roll. 'It's like putting Elastoplast on,' said the bridegroom.

The teacher was pleased to see the children using the gummed paper as she knew they would find this knowledge valuable in the future, when they wanted to fasten cardboard boxes together. The bride's and bridesmaids' heads were measured next. Head-dresses were made from lengths of thin card with beads for decorations. When the teacher heard the children comparing the size of their heads, she used this interest and gradually built up a class record and histogram. The children dressed up and paraded around the school and came back to the house corner to continue their play.

Getting ready for the wedding

Next morning the 'bride' brought a silver horseshoe that she had been given when she was a bridesmaid and the play continued. When she saw the interest was still strong the teacher produced a wedding card and a small wedding-cake box. After these had been examined the children decided they would like to have a 'proper' wedding, with a wedding cake, invitations and party. Silver doilies which the teacher also provided were quickly added to the bouquets and used for decorating the invitations. A boy and girl spent half the morning making a two-tiered wedding-cake from a sweet tin and a biscuit tin which they borrowed from the shop. The teacher wrote out the invitations on the decorated cards and the bride added the names in the name spaces. The groom wrote place name cards. Mother and father made cornflake cakes. The bridesmaids made jellies in small moulds. In the afternoon the bride and bridesmaids dressed up again and after a brief ceremony walked around the school and back to the 'house' where the wedding party was to be held. Mother and father, aided by the best man and the vicar, had arranged two tables with lace curtains as cloths, the wedding cake in the centre of one, name cards, cakes and jellies on the other. There were no additional guests; only the children involved in the play partook of the feast. The next day the bride and bridesmaids collected and made small boxes which they decorated as wedding-cake boxes. They went round the school and copied teachers' names on to a pad; then they asked their own teacher to write down the cook and welfare assistants' names. Later all these people received wedding-cake boxes which had been 'stamped' and posted in the school post-box. Each box was covered by a name label and contained a piece of polystyrene painted brown in the centre to represent the cake. This had been carefully placed on a piece of silver doily. The other children in the group did not continue the play although the teacher noticed that during the rest of the term different children occasionally played at being bride and having a wedding party. The teacher brought a collection of fashion pictures and magazines which she placed with the writing and reading materials. Wedding cards made by the children appeared in the shop. The four girls in the original group wanted to make a book about weddings. They compiled a large scrap-book, decorating the cover with silver bells and bows cut from old wedding cards. A book telling the story of the wedding, the preparations and the feast was written by the teacher at the children's dictation and then illustrated by them. This and the scrap-book became part of the class library for the rest of the term.

When the class was asked what they would next like to have on their display bench they suggested a wedding display. Parents loaned wedding photographs to form a background. The teacher wrote under each one at the owner's suggestion and the class enjoyed reading and examining this exhibition of photographs. After the display had been made the teacher noticed that the 'brides' and 'grooms' began having their photographs taken in 'wedding play'.

Teachers can now:
1 analyse the motivation, learning and development in this play
2 answer the question 'How did the teacher structure this play?'

Our analysis and answers can be found in Appendix 1.

Using Make/Believe Play

1 Provide dressing-up materials that are adaptable and therefore encourage make-believe play.
2 Provide art/craft materials that encourage children to engage in make-believe with the materials they have made or the pictures they have created.
3 Observe all the make/believe play as often as possible with the intention of participating, initiating and intervening where appropriate.
4 Record your objectives for becoming involved.
5 Record the learning and development in the play.

References

MOMMENS, N. (1957) *Polutin and the Red Indians* Faber
UNDERHILL, R. (1970) *The Antelope Singer* Penguin

SAND

WATER

WOOD

Clay

Introduction

We explained earlier that play with natural materials is divided into sensory, imaginative and exploratory. We hope that by now teachers are practised in analysing the descriptions of play given, and will be able to analyse Play with Natural Materials for themselves. These therefore include recordings of the children's and teachers' language and provide detailed accounts of the play. Questions are given for discussion.

Play with sand, water, clay and wood has been described in detail in the following pages, since these are the most common materials in schools. But other natural materials are available; leaves, acorns, beech masts and shells also give rise to symbolic imaginative play, and mud is always a favourite! When the Project teachers explored the immediate environment of the school they often found unexpected sources of materials, e.g. sawdust and chalk. Parents can sometimes offer natural materials that teachers are unable to procure.

All these materials are satisfying for children. They can maltreat or destroy their models without fear of reprimand. The materials respond to rough and gentle treatment, they encourage children to be inquisitive. They can be enjoyed when playing alone. They give rise to cooperative play. They encourage the use of language. One teacher recorded: 'I was amazed that there was so much conversation. In all my observations I had difficulty in writing everything down.'

However all children are not equally attracted to play with natural materials. Some may avoid them because of the mess they create. They do not want to be blamed at home because they return from school with their costly clothes soiled, nor scolded in school because they have smeared expensive books with clay. Teachers do not want to contend with justifiably irate parents and caretakers. Precautions are therefore essential: enveloping overalls must be provided for children to wear. Surfaces that will be harmed or made slippery by water, sand or clay must be protected with some form of covering – layers of newspaper may be the cheapest! Mops, brooms, floorcloths, dustpan and brush must be easily available for cleaning. The means to wash or wipe hands must be close to the play; it may be necessary to bring a bowl of water and paper towels into classrooms that have no sinks. If these protective measures are difficult to provide in a small classroom, teachers might wish to consider having a different play material each day in the week, i.e. dry sand on Monday, wet sand on Tuesday and so on.

Before describing play with sand, water, clay and wood we look at the provision for each of these materials.

Provision of materials

Most schools offer their children the opportunity of playing with both wet and dry sand. Teachers' observations show the different experiences gained, and record that they recognize that both should be provided.

Many teachers in the Project who provided dry sand for the first time were surprised that the children's interest was maintained in playing with it. They had not realized it provided so many possibilities for learning and development.

In some classrooms where space is restricted and two sand trays cannot be provided, teachers have water at hand for the children to add to the dry sand. This gives the group using the sand at the time the experience of dry and wet sand, but another group wanting dry sand obviously has to wait until the sand has dried out. Frequently when the children add water to the sand they do so not merely to moisten the sand but because they are imagining a situation that requires water and sand. The sand tray then becomes 'flooded' and it may take several days to dry the sand. For this reason wherever possible we suggest that the provision of both dry and wet sand is advantageous.

Sand is usually provided in large sand trays for groups of up to four or six children at a time. Sometimes small individual trays are available for children to use on a table or bench; these give the opportunity for children who want to devise an imaginary play situation on their own to play without their sand being disturbed by others. It is also easier to keep individual tray constructions for children to continue their play from one day to another, as other children are not being deprived of the use of large quantities of sand.

Standing or kneeling around a sand tray and using one's hands restricts the kind of play possible. A sand pit that is large enough for a group of children to walk about and play in provides opportunities for different experiences and larger constructions. Some schools are fortunate enough to have large sand pits outside that are not vandalized, in which the children play whenever the weather is fine. Others, not so fortunate, but where the value of a large sand area is recognized, have a sand area on the floor within the classroom; this obviously depends on the space available. Some teachers suspend a plank above the tray for children to put their shapes on or to keep their sand equipment on. Wherever an outside sand pit is provided we would suggest that it should be in constant use. Some schools have difficulty in keeping the sand replenished and clean but those which spend time and money on their outside sand pit find the play merits the expenditure.

Equipment that can be used in sand play includes:

Capacity measures, sand/water wheel, containers of different shapes or sizes for filling and emptying, transparent funnels of different sizes, transparent tubes of different lengths and diameters, transparent sieves of different types and sizes.

Rakes, sand combs and moulds of different patterns and sizes.

Materials for imaginative play, e.g. cars, model animals, Lego, shells, stones, conkers.

WATER

It is important to remember that children have played with water in many natural situations before they come to school: in the bath, in the washbasin, in condensation or rain on window panes, puddles in the street, rain collected in holes in the garden, the overflow from a gutter. They know that hands and face can be dried after washing, that wet clothes dry on the line or in a tumble drier. In schools we provide opportunities for this play to continue.

Many teachers supplement or replace standard water play sets with collections of containers, sieves, sprays, syringes, tubes, and improvised materials for sinking and floating. Some transparent plastic containers and tubing that allow the children to see the flow of water are desirable. Rather than use manufactured sets of boats, teachers often provide their own, or materials with which the children can make boats, e.g. foil pie-cases of different shapes and sizes, to which sails can be attached, or Plasticine that the children can mould into different shapes. They will discover whether shallow boats float better than deep boats, and which materials make effective sails, which are absorbent and which are not.

The choice of water play may be dictated by the amount of space available; it is easier to provide for experiments in water play where protective floor covering is not needed. The playground, covered outdoor areas or courtyards, are obvious places for water play. Schools with swimming or paddling pools are able to offer extra experiences with water. Some teachers have commented that sinks intended for water play are often unsuitable: some are too shallow or narrow; many restrict the size of the group and type of play because they are not freestanding. Colour and soap suds are occasionally added to the water to increase the children's experience and encourage imaginative play.

Play with water that arises in domestic play, e.g. doll washing, clothes washing, cleaning, washing dishes and cooking utensils, has been described in the section on Domestic Play. Given the opportunity, children will often add water to other natural materials. Descriptions of this kind of play are given in the appropriate sections.

CLAY

Teachers' reports reveal that many find clay the messiest and most troublesome natural material children play with in school:

> 'When it gets on the floor, you can't just mop it up, it treads all over the school.'
> 'They get it on their hands, and when they go to wash it off, they leave it on the door handles and taps, everything they touch.'
> 'It needs so much preparation to get it right for them to use.'
> 'You are always having to soften it up, every time they use it.'
> 'I find dough gives the same experience and it's much cleaner.'

Yet those who provide clay believe that its especial properties should be experienced by young children and that it is possible to control the mess. Some teachers are trying out new clays that are advertised as not requiring firing and constant reconstitution. Clay that is the correct consistency for easy moulding makes comparatively little mess on clothes and furniture and should not require the addition of water when it is used. Instructions on preparing and using clay with young children can be found in art and craft books.

When teachers want to give children the chance to discover what happens if water and clay are combined this could occur on special occasions when extra precautions are taken. Clay can be prepared with the assistance of two or three children at a time so that all have the experience in turn. Sometimes infants don't know what it is they are using. Six year olds, Elizabeth and Clare, were discussing the clay which was provided for them once a week.

Elizabeth: What's this?
Clare: It's Plasticine isn't it?
Elizabeth: No, silly, it can't be it's not in lots of colours.
Clare: P'raps it's dough. It feels a bit like it.

Some teachers make a small hole in a lump of clay into which they put water, they leave this resting on a saucer in the centre of the clay bench or table so that the children can moisten a finger. At the same time the water and clay become slip in the saucer and children are able to play with this small amount of slip if they wish and discover what happens when water is added to clay. If children add water to the clay every time they use it, they are prevented from discovering its modelling property. All teachers are agreed that large lumps of clay should be available, so that the children have sufficient to make large models to handle in different ways – pounding, pummelling, rolling, twisting, squeezing.

Teachers always arrange for children to keep their models if they wish; this is the way they discover what happens to clay when it dries and how they must shape it if it is to remain whole. To understand the latter they obviously need an informed adult to help them work out why some pieces fall off and others stay intact. Children may reject clay if they are continually disappointed when their models fall apart and they cannot work out why. Recordings were sent in of 'old hands' explaining to the uninitiated; a seven year old helped a five year old: 'That's too thin there, it'll break when it dries. Let me show you, put this piece on to make it thick; press it in, that's right.' One five year old was heard to say to his friend: 'Don't roll it so thin, it won't lift up. I'm learning you aren't I?'

WOOD

Teachers' recordings reveal children's desire to play with wood, and that they sustain their interest even from one term to the next. They bring wood from home, ask to complete models left unfinished, and are eager to paint and varnish as well as play with them.

All teachers complain about the difficulty of procuring wood for use in schools. Offcuts that were once freely given by saw-mills, if the teachers and children collected them, now seem to be unobtainable. A few schools still have a source of supply and describe wood being burned in wood yards. Unfortunately much that is offered to schools and finds its way into infant classrooms is difficult for children to use in a traditional way. Many teachers comment on the frustration this causes: 'I watched Michael struggling to nail his wood and went to his assistance. I had to admit failure too, the wood kept splitting.' 'When I tried to help I found the wood much too hard.'

Unlike the natural materials described so far wood has the disadvantage that it cannot be re-used. Nails are expensive too! Schools cannot afford to buy sufficient quantities of wood to satisfy the children's desire to construct. They may be forced to use supplies of wood that children cannot saw or nail. Where this happens teachers must revise their preconceived ideas of play with wood. The wood must be fastened with glue instead of nails and sawn into a variety of lengths and shapes by an adult (if necessary with an electric saw) before the children use it. Modern adhesives dry quickly and are obtainable in containers, easy for children to manage. Many teachers show children how to stick wood to prevent them struggling in vain with hammer and nails. Some schools are trying Surform tools as well as sandpaper for smoothing wood.

It is obvious that tools used with wood are dangerous unless the children have been shown how to use them. Teachers are all aware that an adult must demonstrate the correct handling of tools, that children must understand the safety rules and that reminders should be given regularly. Most dangers arise through wood not being held *firmly*, so teachers should insist that all wood being sawn is put in a vice, or held with a bench hook, and wood should be clamped as well. Pincers are dangerous because children try to *pull* out nails by wrestling them with an upward pull. Should a nail come out suddenly there is a danger of the child receiving a blow in the face with the handle of the pincers. If the nail is gripped the handles should be rolled downwards, using the rounded pincer jaws as a fulcrum, the effort is *away* from the child and the nail comes out easily.

The following tools can be used by infants, providing they are shown how to use them. (We strongly advise teachers to consult specialist books on the use and care of tools.)

Saws, tenon, junior hacksaw, Surform type tools, hammers, pincers, drill, screwdrivers, awl, ruler, sandpaper, nails, glue.

The problem of noise when children hammer and saw wood often worries teachers. This type of play is frequently provided for in corridors, courtyards and outdoor play spaces. Where classes are confined to one room, teachers select times when other noisy activities are occurring.

Sensory Play
Sensory play is in some ways the most difficult to record and describe. It is often fleeting and solitary and may not be recognized because some children do not talk about it. Yet it is obvious that both older and younger children enjoy looking, listening, smelling and feeling and are conscious of these sensations when they play with natural materials.

126

DRY SAND

Three five year olds, two boys and a girl, kept interrupting their exploratory play to feel the sand. Their teacher observed it was giving pleasure and experience through the tactile senses. They kept picking up handfuls and letting the sand trickle through their fingers; one kept patting the sand and digging into it.

Two children in a vertically grouped class were playing together in the sand. The older child who had brought to school a book on dinosaurs made holes and small heaps of sand as she invented a story about plant-eaters and meat-eaters:

> Now they are having a fight; the meat-eater is hiding behind this hill, he can't see the plant-eater 'cos he's gone back to his cave. You make a cave for your plant-eater like this.

But the teacher reported her companion 'was more interested in feeling the sand, holding up his hands and letting it run through', so the older child continued her dinosaur game alone.

Three six year olds, two girls and a boy, using a water wheel in dry sand for the first time were so fascinated by the speed of the wheel turning that they could not be distracted but spent over ten minutes pouring the dry sand on the wheel and watching it revolve.

WET SAND

Reception class children have often been recorded using their hands to pile up 'castles' with damp sand and spending a long time patting their constructions. Observed carefully, they do not appear to be mending cracks or moulding the shape of the castle but rather experiencing the feel of the sand and the rhythm of the movement.

A seven year old boy in an outside sand pit was covering his legs and feet with sand when the welfare assistant commented, 'You've been doing that a long time, haven't you Gary?'
'Yes, I like to feel it slipping off – it goes slowly.'

Two six year olds, barefoot in the outside sand pit, were walking from side to side laughing as they scrunched their toes.

Ellen: It feels funny, it's scratchy.
David: No it isn't, it's tickly.
Ellen: It itches me.

WATER

Two girls and two boys aged five and six were observed by their teacher. She reported, 'the sheer joy of feeling the bubbles, blowing them and lifting them out of the water was enough to hold their interest for fifteen minutes – there was a good deal of sharing the pleasure of the feel of the soapy water'.

A five year old girl was floating a hollow ball in a jug of water. She sank the ball laughing as the air bubbled out. She emptied the water out and began again, laughing each time the water 'glugged' into the ball.

Two five year old boys were playing with detergent bottles, one said, 'Bubbles, lots of them, feel them, look at the bubbles, lots of them all around.'

Children often remark about the noise water makes, like the five year old who said, 'I like the pouring sound.'

A seven year old boy called others to hear his water song as he blew through different sized tubing. Another said, 'It's making a trickly noise.'

A group of girls, asked what they thought water felt like, volunteered, 'It's squeezy – it's slippery, it's soft, it's smooth.'

No wonder children find water play so fascinating. After she had washed the dolls, a six year old said, 'My hands have gone all wobbly!'

CLAY

As with other natural materials teachers have found it difficult to record children's sensory play with clay. When they observe them stroking, smoothing, slapping, pummelling, and patting the clay for long periods, they comment on the children's enjoyment and apparent satisfaction in the feel of the material. Some teachers have asked the children what clay feels like, but obviously their replies are limited by their vocabulary. Unless the children express their feelings spontaneously one can only conjecture their reaction to the materials.

A seven year old girl was observed smoothing the clay very gently for five minutes after she had destroyed her model of a girl dressed in a 'swirly skirt'. Was she unaware of her actions and the clay, or was she enjoying the feel of the material? In a group of five year olds making a variety of models and describing imaginary situations involving them, one girl sat squeezing clay with her fingers for ten minutes. Was she conscious of the clay and her movements or merely listening to her companions' conversation?

Jean, Peter and Tom, all six years old, talked about the clay as they dipped their hands in water and smoothed them over the clay.

Jean: Feel it – it's silky.
Peter: Mine's smoothy.
Tom: It's getting to feel warm. It was cold when we started. Now it's warm.

A teacher who asked two five year olds what they thought about the clay they had used for the first time was told:
'It had a lovely squashy feel.'
'It had a cold feel.'
Another group of five year olds offered:
'It's slippery.'
'It's slimy.'
'It's pattery.'
'It's like cement.'
A teacher questioned five year old Graham as he picked up a piece of clay for the first time.

Teacher: What does it feel like?
Graham: Very soft.
Teacher: Is it heavy or light?
Graham: It's very soft.

It could be argued that these examples are often describing exploratory rather than sensory play. Are children who have had many opportunities to play with clay, and have often made models, still exploring its potential when they stroke and pat it?

WOOD

Some seven year old girls were emptying a sack of wood pieces into a box.

Susan: Smell it. I like it, do you?
Phyllis: I can smell it when my dad's cutting it with his electric drill, he makes a lot of sawdust.
Rachel: We made a bonfire with the wood when my mum had cut the hedge, wood doesn't half smell when you burn it.

A group of children had been to the beach and brought back a collection of driftwood. As they unpacked their holdalls they discussed the shape, colour and feel of the wood.

Tracey: Look at this it looks like a fish. That mark's like its eye. Feel it – it's smooth.

Russell:	I know – feel these pieces they're all smooth. It feels like they've been sandpapered.
Robert:	They're all silky.
Deborah:	Look at the lines on this bit – it looks like waves.
Tracey:	Look, this one's got a proper pattern.
Deborah:	A tree's got round lines like that when it's chopped down.
Russell:	All wood's got patterns on it hasn't it?
Tina:	I like this shape – feel it.
Robert:	Pooh – it smells rotten.

A five year old boy was described as being 'fascinated by the sawdust as his friends sawed'. He picked it up from the floor and trickled it through his fingers, saying, 'It's like snow.'

As teachers have read these typical examples of sensory play with natural materials they will have realized that sensory play occurs in all categories of play. Children are aware of all the materials they use in Domestic, Construction and Make/Believe play. If teachers wish to develop sensory play they need to be conscious of the possibilities in all the children's play.

We suggest teachers answer these questions about the sensory play descriptions and then ask similar questions about the play in their own classrooms.

1   What are the children doing in these examples of sensory play?
2   What kind of learning and development is taking place?
3   What form should the teacher's involvement have taken?
4   How could she have shown the children she appreciates these sensory experiences?
5   How could she have encouraged them in this sensory awareness?
6   Is it possible to develop these sensory play experiences in any of the children's other classroom activities?
7   What would be the teacher's objectives in encouraging sensory play?

Imaginative Play

Teachers reported as many examples of imaginative play as exploratory play, and it was often difficult to separate them. Many examples overlap and are open to different interpretations.

Sometimes children have no tools or materials other than the sand and their hands; more often they use sand tools and containers or small toys to aid their play. In some instances the softness and flow of the sand inspires the imagination and the children then develop a make-believe story or sequence of events based on a television series, a film, a story they know, or an experience they have had.

Six year old Elsie was observed playing with sand in a shallow individual sand tray. She made small piles of sand in different parts of the tray, traced paths with her fingers and kept moving a small pile of sand around. When the teacher asked her what she was doing Elsie said, 'A little girl lives here.' She pointed to one pile of sand.

> She's got a kitten that plays here with her in the garden, but it got out when the little girl wasn't looking, and ran away and got lost. The little girl is looking for her kitten; she's going to the police station.

She moved her finger along one of the 'paths' to another pile of sand.

> The kitten isn't here. She's going to ask if her nan knows where it is. She's going into her nan's garden. She's found her kitten under this pile of grass cuttings in the corner. Her nan's putting the kitten in a basket with a lid on and they're taking it back home. Now the little girl's pouring some milk in a saucer and the kitten's drinking it. Now the little girl's going for her tea.

Elsie let the sand fall through her fingers on to the tray to represent the milk pouring.

While this story was being recited another six year old girl at the same table was making a garden in her sand tray using shells and conkers. She paid no attention to the first child's play and conversation. The teacher when questioned knew of no story that Elsie had been told that resembled her account, and Elsie explained, 'I just told it myself, no, I haven't got a kitten but I have got a nan – the little girl went to the police station because that's where you go when you're lost.'

Whether this six year old was recounting a known story or inventing one, she was following a sequence from beginning to end and inventing situations in the sand. She needed the sympathetic interest and questioning of an adult to encourage her to use language to describe and explain her story.

Further dialogue might have discussed where else the kitten could have hidden, why it went under the grass cuttings, and how the little girl felt when she was searching for her pet. It was obvious that this six year old had learned how to sustain dialogue and reason since she volunteered the statement 'that's where you go when you're lost'. The adult could therefore have fostered her language development, and possibly her future play, by further dialogue of this kind continued for as long as interest remained. She could have encouraged her to imagine the different emotions of the kitten, the little girl and the grandmother, to work out the possible solutions to their problems and to speculate about courses of action open to them.

In contrast to Elsie's originally silent play, a rising-five year old girl talked continually to herself as she played in a sand trough, pushing it into small piles and picking them up and putting them in a bucket.

> I'm making a cake and I'm putting it in the oven – now it's in the oven – now it's done – I'm making another cake – here it's going in the oven – I'm making lots of cakes.

This was play that was both imitative and symbolic and apparently quite spontaneous; it required no assistance and no equipment except the bucket! An adult could have discussed with this five year old what kind of cakes she was making and how she was regulating the heat in the oven. But as this play was so quick and the child young, questions and discussions might not have been appropriate. It might have been better in this instance, since the child's language and play seemed to be simple and rapid, to see if the example of an adult playing alongside would help her to be more imaginative and to sustain her play. The result might not be immediately obvious but could produce more extended play later on in another situation, e.g. in domestic play. One way in which the adult might play:

> I think I'll make some cakes too – I'm making a large coconut cake – here's the flour – I need four large scoops of flour and two of sugar, may I borrow some? Now I want a small quantity of coconut, I think one of these little spoons, just level, will be sufficient, I'll put a cherry on top in a circle. When I've finished I'm going to make some jam tarts – I'll make them in a row like this.

This is a good example of the kind of 'parallel' adult play described on page 22.

132

Several observations record children imagining volcanic eruptions in their dry sand play. It is possible that a television programme or a film may have stimulated this play but the way in which dry sand behaves obviously reminds both boys and girls of what they have seen. One six year old Japanese boy trickling sand into the tray through his fingers said, 'Here's a sandstorm – it's over a volcano.' Then added, as he moved his hands around in the tray, 'This is the lava – look it's erupting. Now here's a cave.' He made a hole in the sand with his fingers pushing it aside, 'The horses and men are frightened – they hide in this cave.'

Two six year old girls talking as they pushed their hands under the sand were heard to say, 'Look it's moving like the ground round a volcano – look the ground breaks.' An adult passing by commented, 'Yes, it's crumbling, isn't it.'

This type of play gives the children opportunities:

1   to recall events they have watched or experienced; 'the visual image remains vague if it cannot be drawn or mimed' (Piaget 1951)
2   to control situations in the symbolism of play, where certain objects are consciously represented by others
3   to resolve the situation with a happy ending as when the horses and men hid in a cave to escape the lava
4   to predict what might happen if . . . , how someone might behave if . . . , how someone would feel if . . .
5   to realize the need to string together an ordered sequence of events, to recall a story or experience accurately
6   to foster language development, reading and writing
7   to experience in play, situations which provide vivid material for writing and reading.

WET SAND

A reception class boy was playing with small plastic animals in the sand tray. He buried the animals, then indicated the base of the tray which he had scraped clean and informed his companion: 'This is the sea; these are the caves and the crocodile is hiding. You hold this one. You say "come out there".' His companion repeated the words, but then devised her own activity so he continued to play alone, fighting and hiding the animals in the caves. It was interesting that this young boy did not need water to represent the sea and was able to develop his make-believe play, probably drawing on a story or pictures in a book, or from watching television. No adult was involved and the play continued for ten minutes. He talked to himself throughout the time and did not refer to his companion again.

Two six year old boys had covered several Dinky cars in the sand and smoothed the sand carefully on top. Then they built a road, making it go down the side of the mound, explaining to each other, 'It's got to be smooth for the cars to run down'. After the road was finished they told their teacher it was a motorway and the flat bit was a flyover. When they wanted to move the cars along the road they remembered that they had buried them. The teacher asked how they could get them out without completely dismantling the road. After some hesitation one boy went to get a stick from the brick box and started to dig holes in the flat part pushing the stick down into the sand. He explained, 'I'm making holes so I can look down them and find the car there and get it out.' When he saw the sand covered with holes, he said, 'It just looks like a bees' house in my sister's book.'

In both these examples, the material aided the make-believe, and may have given rise to it. The play started with burying the animals and the cars, then the situation developed. All three boys talked as they played, explaining the play to themselves and, in the second example, to each other. Once the two boys realized they had a problem, they solved it by drawing on previous experience. They knew that they could make a hole in wet sand, that it would not collapse and that they could see down it. They evidently did not know how to use the stick as a probe. It was not recorded whether they made this discovery.

WATER

Six year olds Ronald and Fred, playing in the paddling pool, noticed that they were making footprints; they immediately started a stalking game. Fred said, 'I'm an Indian and I'm following your footprints – I'm crawling along.' Ronald ran in and out of the pool making footprints, but when the stalker was upon him he jumped into the pool, and announced, 'You can't follow me now 'cos I'm not making footprints in the water. I'm in a lake, I've got to the other side and you can't find me.'

Seven year olds Alison, Myra and Caroline had put all the squeezy bottles in the water trough; they played with them until they had soap bubbles covering the surface.

Alison: We've made all this washing-up liquid. It can be a washing-up liquid factory. Let's put all the bottles in a line here on the floor – we'll fill them with this funnel and you can put the lids on.

Myra:	If you don't work quicker you won't get your wages.
Caroline:	Hope we don't use all the water before they're all filled up.
Alison:	Don't worry there's plenty here and when we've finished we can open a shop and sell them.

Children often liken water falling through a sieve or spray to rain. One teacher recorded a five year old boy playing with first a sieve, then a colander and finally a bucket, saying, 'It's raining slowly. Now I'm making a storm. This is going to be a thunderstorm.' A mother passing by remarked, 'I'd call it a deluge!'

The boy was using experience gained in previous water play, of the flow of water from the sieve, the colander and bucket, and combining it with his knowledge of rainfall. Did he think a thunderstorm caused heavier rainfall than a storm or was he referring to the noise of water falling from the upturned bucket? Did he gain satisfaction from controlling the rainfall?

Much of the imaginative play with water is concerned with children's experience of floating and sinking.

A five year old boy balanced a ping-pong ball on top of a larger ball with holes in it and said, 'It's a snowman – it's floating – it's sinking – the sun has melted it.' Here we have recall of sun melting snow, the comparison of the melting snowman disappearing and the sinking balls being submerged.

Four six year old boys were playing with soldiers, rafts and tanks, in a water tray that contained two large stones referred to as islands. The soldiers were attacking the enemy hiding on the islands. Some swam under water, others were frogmen hiding bombs in the caves, some fell off the tank when it exploded and were drowned. A few tried to climb up the rocks round the islands but slipped off into the water and had to be rescued by the rafts. Although this play was accompanied by shooting and explosion noises there was no bombing, it was confined to swimming, drowning and sailing.

These examples of play involved:

1 cooperation
2 observation
3 incorporation of observation in a make-believe situation
4 development of a make-believe situation
5 dialogue
6 recall of knowledge gained from television, film and story
7 reasoning.

Teachers' observations show how satisfying clay is, in that a child can rapidly change it from a snake to a crocodile and a snail in a matter of minutes, and yet spend half an hour meticulously putting the spikes one at a time on a hedgehog. It has the advantage that children feel in complete control of the material. Sometimes the shape the clay takes seems to inspire the play, as when a five year old girl banged the clay into a sausage shape and picking it up wriggled it saying, 'It's a snake – ee – ee – ee.'

At other times the fact that the shape of the clay does not resemble the imagined object is no deterrent to the child's symbolism. Several small clay sausages were identified as soldiers around whom was woven a lengthy story by their five year old creator.

Three boys and a girl, aged six, shared each other's play and conversation for twenty-five minutes.

Colin:	Is that a man?
Mark:	Yes. This is his head. (He was rolling some clay into a ball.) I'm going to do his neck next. (He had already made the body and legs.)
Colin:	I'm going to make a spaceship. What are you making Andrew?
Andrew:	A nest. It's got eggs inside. It's got seven eggs in it. Are you making a mushroom or a tree Suzanne?
Suzanne:	It's a tree. I'm making a pond now. (She flattened out a circular piece of clay on the table and then began to make some small balls.)
Teacher:	What are you going to put on the pond?
Suzanne:	I'm going to use these balls as stones and put them all round the pond.
Teacher:	Why?
Suzanne:	To make it look pretty.
Andrew:	I'm making a tree now to put the nest in. I forgot to make the tree. How am I going to make it?
Suzanne:	Break it (the nest) all up and make a nest the right size to fit in the tree.
	(Andrew squeezed the nest up in his hands.)
Andrew:	The eggs are still not cracked. I squeezed the nest and they still aren't cracked. (He then began to make another nest.)

Mark:	I'm making a dinosaur. The man is looking for bones of dinosaurs.
Andrew:	I've got to make a little nest now to fit in the tree.
Suzanne:	I'm making another tree.
	(Andrew began making eggs for the new nest counting them as he made them. He made seven as before. He then put the nest on top of the tree.)
Andrew:	It's too big, I'll have to make another one and make it smaller.
Colin:	I'm going to make a nest. (He then made some eggs.) I've got ten eggs in my nest.
	(Andrew began to make a bigger tree. Meanwhile Suzanne made some more trees and Mark was getting on with his dinosaur.)
Colin:	I'm going to make a garden. (He squashed up his nest.) My garden is going to have trees in it.
Teacher:	What else do you have in a garden?
Colin:	Trees, flowers, grass.
Teacher:	How are you going to make the grass?
Colin:	I don't know yet.
Mark:	I know. You get tiny bits of clay and stick them on to the table like this.
	(Colin began to make a tree as the other two had done, making a sausage for the trunk and a ball for the leaves and branches.)
	(Mark had now made the body of his dinosaur and was making the head. The dinosaur had a large open mouth and he made some pointed teeth. When this was finished, he joined the head to the body.)
Andrew:	I'm putting a wall round the tree so that bears and foxes can't get the eggs.
Teacher:	Can bears and foxes get over the wall?
Andrew:	No.
Teacher:	Why not?
Andrew:	'Cos it's too high.
Teacher:	Can foxes and bears jump?
Andrew:	Foxes can, but bears can't. Bears can climb trees, but not over walls. I've left a little hole so that when a fox tries to climb up the wall, he'll get his foot stuck in the hole.
	(Andrew then took another piece of clay and began to make it flat.)

Andrew: Do you know how I make the clay flat? I don't need hands. I go like that. (He banged his arm on the clay.) Look I've made patterns with my jumper. I don't need patterns, so I smooth it out with my fingers.

Suzanne: I'm making some grass now. (She had already made four trees and a pond.)

Colin: What's that Mark?

Mark: It's a dinosaur. I saw it in a museum. They stuck skin on it after they found the bones, to show us what they looked like.

Andrew: Is that in a museum?

Mark: Yes.

(Mark continued putting the finishing touches on his dinosaur. It was about eight inches long and four inches tall. The man he made earlier was about two inches tall.)

This play has been described at length because it is not only an example of cooperation in imaginative play but also of the learning involved.

It can be analysed for:

1 mathematical content
2 language content
3 child interaction
4 reasoning
5 problem solving
6 teacher involvement.

Five seven year olds planned their play when they started.

Malcolm: All the girls make dinner and we'll make cups and plates. Yes, we're having sausages and chips, I'm making a plate and afterwards I'll do a cup. We're the husbands and you're the wives.

Sandra: Right, how many sausages do you like, four? No, more than that, five, six, seven sausages, nine, ten, eleven, twelve?

Fiona: You need a lot for husbands. I'm just going to make a lid for this teapot, you forgot the lid Ian. Look I've made a birthday cake – it's very big.

Malcolm:	You make a big oven and I'll do a saucepan. I've got to make it round first.
Donald:	He's making the oven and I'm making another saucepan – the cooker I mean – no oven's right. I'm making it much, much bigger.
Malcolm:	My saucepan is a non-sticky saucepan.
Ian:	This plate's big enough for dinner. Three eggs today.
Fiona:	It's a birthday cake – there's a candle on my birthday cake.
Ian:	Look at my dinner – sausages and eggs.

How does this example of cooperative imaginative play compare with the previous one?

1   Is there as much mathematical learning?
2   Is the language content different?
3   Is the child interaction different?
4   Is as much reasoning required?
5   Is there any problem solving?
6   Could an adult have been involved?
7   Is the imaginative content the same or different (excluding the obvious difference in subject)?

WOOD

Sometimes children know what they want to make with wood and appear to develop their imaginative ideas as they play.

A five year old boy announced that he was going to make the Star Ship Enterprise. He talked and played as he hammered, sawed and glued:

I'll put a wheel here, now I can steer. This nail's to keep the rain out, if it's like that the rain gets in. Here's another nail, that's for the sun. Push it like that, that's right, now a bit of sun's coming in. I want a bit of wood for them to stand on. I'll find a bit – this'll do. Mmm, now they've disappeared.

Afterwards when he was discussing his ship with his teacher he insisted that a large nail in the centre was to stop the flies coming in. His companion who had been playing silently talked to the teacher about his boat.

139

Teacher: Is this the sail? (She pointed to a sail shaped block of wood in the centre.)

Robin: No, it's a fish boat. You see you catch the fish and that bit (the supposed sail) is where the fish go.

Teacher: How do you get the fish up there?

Robin: You throw them up there and then they slide down here.

Teacher: What happens to them when they get into the bottom of the boat?

Robin: You cook them – they're all cooking in here – it's a big kitchen.

Teacher: Do you eat them all on the boat?

Robin: No, there's too many, you take some back home.

At other times children shape and hammer, exploring the tools and the wood. The results stimulate their imagination.

A six year old girl had smoothed a block of wood with sandpaper and knocked three nails in the side. She exclaimed, 'Oh! Look, it's a television.' She pressed the nails and sat back saying, 'Up a little, no down, stop, right, up again, stop, now fire.' Another nail was pressed: 'Look at all the wonderful prizes we have tonight. Who's going to win this lovely caravan?' The teacher heard and said, 'Do the nails go in when you press them?' The girl answered, 'No, it's only pretend.' A boy watching explained: 'They won't go in 'cos you can't press them hard enough. You have to hit them hard with a hammer to make them go in.' The girl laughed: 'You silly – they're not nails – they're the knobs on my television, you don't have to hit *them* with a hammer.'

The teachers on the Project were surprised to discover how imaginative was the children's play with wood. Until they observed, many had thought the children's play merely developed manipulative skills and expertise in using the material and tools. When they talked to the children and observed their play they found how often children had been evolving imaginative ideas as they fashioned the wood. If teachers join in the play they are able to help the children develop and give expression to these ideas. If they are unable to join in but find time to talk to the children about their completed models, they can ask open-ended questions that encourage the children to describe their imaginative ideas. Thus they may be able to suggest ways in which the models can be incorporated into other forms of play.

Teachers could now ask themselves these questions:

1 In the example with the Enterprise and the fishing boat could the teacher have incorporated this imaginative play into the children's reading and writing activities, and if so how?
2 In the example of the girl making the television could the teacher have participated in the play instead of asking questions?
3 If so, how could she have joined in and could her involvement have furthered the learning and development?

Exploratory Play

DRY SAND

Two five year old boys were using a fine meshed sieve over a bucket. First they held it high and low and watched the flow of sand. Kevin said, 'Look, now it's coming out fast, now it's filling my bucket, quickly, oooh, it's going all over the sides of my bucket, hold it lower, then it'll go in. Let me have it now. You pour now.'

Next, they poured different amounts of sand into the sieve and Martin said, 'Put more in now, – a lot, a lot, look it's coming fast – now it's slow – it's finished – yes, it's empty – do it again.'

The teacher who was watching their play suggested they look for some other sieves to pour through. They found a smaller nylon sieve and a much larger meshed sieve with a wooden rim. With the teacher's help they collected more containers to sieve the sand into, and then continued their play for approximately fifteen minutes.

Learning that resulted from this exploratory play
1 The boys discovered
   (a) the flowing property of sand
   (b) how fine it was in texture
   (c) how the sand flowed more quickly through the wide-holed sieve
   (d) how they could control and direct the flow into a container
   (e) how too much sand in the sieve would spill over the container
   (f) how they needed to match the size of the container they were pouring from, to the size of the container they were trying to fill.
2 They compared the sieves for their depth, the size of the mesh, their circumference.
3 They were made aware of the different shape and volume of the containers they were using.

4 Finally, the children commented on the large grains of sand that were left in the bottom of the fine sieve but went through the coarse sieve. From previous sand and water play or other experience they already had the concept of full, half-full and empty, quick and slow. They learned the meaning of two new words: trickle, sprinkle.

Two seven year old girls were using a sieve in the dry sand that had been used earlier in the wet sand. They noticed that the dry sand would not go through quickly and one said to the other, 'Look the dry sand sticks to the wet and won't go through – shake it – see, it makes a different pattern, it's different from the dry sand when it falls through.'

The teacher overheard this comment and asked the girls if they would like to try playing with different sieves and patterns. She suggested they collect as many different utensils as they could use for sprinkling patterns. They spent the rest of the morning collecting sprinklers and spraying patterns with them in the sand. Amongst their collection were salt and pepper pots, a tea strainer, a sugar sifter, a flour sifter, plant pots, colanders, various sizes of funnels including a pie-crust funnel, a piece of wide-meshed curtain net, and narrow-mesh wire netting. They began by trying to pour sand through all of them and watching the flow. Then they made patterns and pictures on the dry sand already in the tray. Next they scraped the sand in the tray to one side and made patterns and pictures on the base of the tray. They tried adding a few drops of water at a time to the sand. They discovered what happened to their patterns if the sand was moist, and how moist the sand must be when it failed to come through the holes in their sieves. Moving over to the wet sand trough they smoothed a base and poured dry sand on wet sand. The teacher asked them if they had tried any other materials in their sieves. They hadn't, but collected small quantities of salt, sawdust, sugar, flour, wood, and lead shavings from the pencil sharpener to experiment with. This play continued into the afternoon and during the next day, and interested several children in the class who were aware of what was happening. With the teacher's encouragement, the girls talked, drew and wrote about their play and discoveries. Later in the week, they made a collection of different materials and pressed them in the sand to see what kind of patterns they made and compared the results in flour and moist sand. They moved the materials like combs over the sand to vary the patterns. One of the girls painted many different and attractive patterns afterwards. Eventually they joined two boys to make their own sieves with muslin and different net curtains.

Learning that resulted from this exploratory play

1 The girls reinforced their knowledge of the differences in the flow of wet and dry sand and the difference between fine and thick substances and varied textures.
2 They discovered the need for different sized sieves and utensils for pouring.
3 They began to understand the process of riddling and purifying by filtering.
4 They were able to translate their play into painting, drawing, reading and writing, and they discovered the need to recall and record accurately and in sequence. They used the word 'fine' in a new way and acquired new vocabulary such as mesh, sieve, riddle, sifter, texture and coarse.

These two examples have been described in some detail because of their similarity, and the way they illustrated the exploratory play of five year olds and seven year olds. The play began in the same way but developed differently, because of the difference in manipulative skill, experience and ability to reason of the older children. For these reasons, the teacher made many more suggestions to the older children. She knew they were able to sustain their interest much longer, and that her suggestions would be incorporated into their play. She was able to make these suggestions because she had observed their play, realized its possibilities, and knew what previous experience the children had in sand play. She did not attempt to set up scientific experiments, but provided the materials and suggestions that would enable the children to make the discoveries in their play. She encouraged them to discuss their discoveries with her, and among themselves, and to record what happened by writing, drawing and recording on a tape, depending on their interest and ability.

Very many other instances of exploratory play were recorded for the Project, all of which would be familiar to teachers who have observed children playing with dry sand. They included simple experiments like putting a finger over the hole of a funnel to see what happened to the flow, to more complicated play using funnels and a mug. In this latter experiment the sand was poured into the cup through the wide end of the funnel and then through the narrow end. Then it was poured through a second funnel into the first and into the cup. Finally the two narrow ends of the funnels were placed together one on top of the other and the sand poured through into the cup. The funnels were repeatedly lifted up to see how much more sand was required to fill the cup. The child who carried out this experiment had already experienced pouring too much sand into a utensil and causing it to overflow. In order to carry out this play the child had to find two funnels that were the same size and a cup that fitted

Exploratory play with dry sand using funnels and a mug

WET SAND

Two boys, one aged six and one seven, were trying to make a tunnel and a hill for their play with model cars. Both children concentrated very hard to get the holes and the slope right. Their first attempt to make the tunnel caused the hill to collapse. One then instructed the other:

> Don't you press your side yet – it was too high before – it may fall down on top of you – make it lower – go very carefully – look what you've done – it's breaking – I'll try pressing it gently – it's mended – now see if it's gone right through. Can you make a hole in the top and touch my hand underneath – it's too soft, put a bit more water in – not too much – see if you can make it firmer – that's right – now try – put your hand in now.

Later when they had made a track over the hill and tunnel, they pushed different sizes of cars along their road. After the hill had collapsed a few times, they were able to discriminate: 'No, don't bring that one up – it's too heavy – only the little ones can go this way.'

Initially this play needed no tools or equipment other than the sand and water and the children's hands. The play and the material set the problem for them and they were able to draw on their previous experience of playing in wet sand to work out the solution. They knew that:

1   the higher their tunnel was, the more likely it was to collapse
2   they needed to proceed slowly watching the sand for cracks and subsidence
3   water added to sand that was crumbling would make it more suitable for moulding
4   too much water would make the sand unsuitable for their purpose.

Note that water was available and that they were accustomed to add water as required; they must have had the experience of making sand too wet to mould and use for building. This discovery is sometimes denied to children in school because of the mess it causes and the time taken for sand to dry. Nevertheless in addition to consolidating knowledge already gained they were still exploring the properties of sand:

1   They had to experiment to find out how large a tunnel they could make in the hill. If they had needed a larger tunnel would they have made a larger hill or would they have abandoned their building?
2   They tried 'pressing the crack gently to see if it would mend'. Previous experience suggested the need for 'gentleness' in manipulating the sand, but they were not sure of the result when they started. Was there any transfer here from their experience in mending cracks in clay? Many more experiences would be required to discover that not all cracks in sand will mend if pressed gently.
3   It is not clear from their dialogue whether they knew from previous exploratory play that a hole from the top would meet a hole from the bottom; were they only discovering if it was possible to do it on this occasion, or were they simply finding out whether their hands would touch?
4   Playing with cars and being frustrated by the collapse of their

roadway made them aware of the different weight of the model cars. They discovered that the largest was not necessarily the heaviest and that they must estimate the weight before they moved the cars over the hill.

A five year old had played with dry sand in the morning using a carton with holes in the side. In the afternoon he had a similar carton in the wet sand; he filled the carton with sand, pressing it firmly and pushing hard on the top. Finally he came to the teacher.

Bill: Look, it won't come out of the holes.
Teacher: I wonder why it won't come out?
Bill: Because it gets stuck – it's not soft, I can push it out with my finger, can I?
Teacher: Try and see if you can.

A group of five year olds, three girls and two boys, had taken the water wheel from the water to the sand. They had never played with it before. One boy struggled to make the wheel work with wet sand. When asked why it wasn't working he said that there was too much sand at the top and he would have to take a little out to make it work. When this failed, the second boy emptied the top, used a spoon to drop the sand through on to the wheel and then poked the sand through the hole with his finger. The girl announced that it wasn't working properly because 'the sand should fall on the tray at the bottom'.

These five year olds were obviously at a much earlier stage of exploratory play with wet sand. They had not the experience of the older children that wet sand would not flow; they probably would not have added water to sand to make it firmer, as the boys did in the previous example. The first five year old, having had the opportunity to use dry sand as well as wet, seems to have been nearer understanding why the wet sand didn't flow – 'It gets stuck – it's not soft'. The teacher might have tried to see if he was ready, by comparing the flow of the dry and the wet sand, and by making sandpies with dry and wet sand with him. She would then have been able to tell whether he was ready to comprehend the reason why they behaved differently, or if he needed much more experience. The second group might have been helped if they could have played with the wheel in dry sand. (Is it an added difficulty that water flows and dry sand flows, but a mixture of the two doesn't?) The teacher's observations suggest that an adult could have discussed and compared with the first child, to see if he was ready to understand why the materials behaved differently. The adult needed to be aware of the futility of pressing the solution, or attempting to explain it verbally, if the child's experience was still too limited. The child needed more play as well as the assistance of an adult. The group appear to have needed much more experience of pouring and sifting before being ready to understand fluidity and viscosity.

WATER

Much of the exploratory play with water that is concerned with fluidity is similar to play with dry sand. Children pour water from one container to another, use funnels and sieves, fill and empty utensils of different sizes and shapes. Like the five year olds playing with sieves and dry sand, a five year old boy playing with water and a sieve told his companion, 'The water comes out here slowly and stays a little while but it won't stay in the colander, look, the holes are too big. When you get it up the water's disappeared.'

A six year old girl filling a jug exclaimed, 'Look, if you put your hand in when this is full, it spills out – see the water goes down.'

Other exploratory play in water, such as floating and sinking play, cannot occur with dry sand. A teacher had placed different lengths of foam rubber near the water. Some six year olds were floating the shorter lengths; one picked up a long length and said, 'I bet this won't float, it's too long.' After they had placed it in the water, another commented, 'I knew it would 'cos it's light.' Another added, 'It's got air in, that's why.'

Five year olds Stephen and Richard were filling different sized yoghurt cartons. When they went for more, Stephen discovered that they floated as he put them in the water. Richard, pouring from a small watering can, said, 'Oh, this one's still floating, and I've put some water in it.' Stephen suggested, 'See if you can sink it with more water. Yes, look it will stand up in the bottom now it's full.'

A teacher observed three seven year olds floating small pieces of paper, cardboard and material that were left over from the boys' experiments with sails on their boats. She suggested that they make a collection of different materials from the collage trolley and see which floated. They filled a box with feather, wood shavings, conkers, beech masts, shells, spaghetti, cotton reels, nails, pieces of bark, corks, cartons, bottle tops, corrugated cardboard, and played with them in the water. With the teacher's help they drew up a chart of things that float and things that sink, which they put on the display board with a notice asking the other children to help them to add to it.

A five year old girl played alone for a long time, pouring water onto a sponge and squeezing it. When her teacher finally decided to join her the girl spoke about the change in the colour of the wet and dry sponge as well as its absorbent quality. She had discovered that the sponge only had a limited capacity.

Five seven year old boys had made small boats with balsa wood, and were playing with them in the water trough. They were disappointed because the sails they had made from material were soaked when the boats turned over. They started to argue about materials that didn't soak up water: 'Well my sister's boots let the water in and my wellies don't.' The teacher joined in their discussion and encouraged them to try as many materials as they could find and to make a chart with two columns – one for materials that absorb water and one for materials that repel water. Two of the boys continued their interest and read about ways in which some animals and birds protect themselves from water. Three girls watched the boys play with water-repellent materials, and after talking about lump sugar disappearing in tea, asked the teacher if they could find out what dissolved in water. A visiting mother helped with these experiments because the girls knew that sometimes they needed hot water.

Many teachers' observations reported children being puzzled by finding that when they poured water into a container that had a hole in the base some of the water remained, and discovering that they had to tip the container to empty it completely. Often the children shake the container to make sure there is water remaining. These observations reinforced teachers in the need to provide some transparent containers for water play.

Two six year old boys, David and Timothy, were pouring water through a funnel into a bent tube that they had attached to a bottle; they were surprised that no water came into the bottle. When they tipped the tube the water flowed into the bottle. The teacher observing, asked them why they thought water hadn't come out. Timothy pointed to the bend and explained that the water had got stuck there. David said, 'Water doesn't go up the tube.'

A five year old boy pushed a tin with a hole in the base into the water trough and shouted: 'Look what I'm making the water do. It's a fountain.'

Two seven year old girls held an inverted funnel under the water with a finger over its end. They then called to the teacher to come and watch the bubbles come up. They asked what was happening and with her help worked out that the air was being pushed out by the water.

148

Two seven year old boys and a girl were playing with some lengths of rubber tubing, a bucket and the water trough. They were taking turns at sucking water into the tube and directing the tube into the bucket, and kept giving each other instructions. After watching the play for a while and seeing that the children were growing frustrated, the teacher went to enquire what they were doing. They said they were trying to get the water to go from the trough along the tube and into the bucket. The teacher said, 'Well let's find out what is happening. Try with plastic tubing.' One boy sucked the water up the tube while the other children watched carefully and reported what was happening to the water. They discovered that the water came up the tube when they sucked at the top, but it always slipped back again when they stopped sucking. The girl, Sarah, said, 'Well, I know you can do it because my dad got some petrol out of his car and put it in a can for my uncle, 'cos he'd run out of petrol.' The teacher asked Sarah if she had watched her dad, and receiving an affirmative answer, suggested that she tell them very carefully exactly what he did. Sarah said, 'He put a rubber pipe into the petrol tank and sucked it. When he put the end of the pipe into the can, the petrol filled it up.'

The teacher suggested they try this and the experiment went on;

'How did dad get petrol from his car into uncle's car?'

but they still had no success. Finally, since none of the children was able to find the clue, the teacher asked Sarah, 'Was dad standing up?'

'No, kneeling on a mat with his face near the can. He got petrol in his mouth.'

They tried, and at last the water ran into the bucket. They continued to play for a long time watching the water run up and down the tube, and finding out when it stopped running into the bucket. Finally, at the suggestion of one of the boys, they used a narrower tube and compared the flow of water.

Two five year olds, floating cotton reels in a trough, were enthralled to see that when they poured water through a tube into the trough, the cotton reels spun round. Similarly, a six year old, using a wooden cheesebox as a boat in a war game, shouted, 'Look, it's got in a whirlpool', when the box came into water that was being forced round by another child pouring through a funnel.

Seven year olds, William, James and Richard, were playing together. William held a large plastic tube while James pumped water through it. After a while, Richard fitted a bottle lid over the end of the tube; they called to the teacher to come and see.

James: Look, the water is so strong it pushes the lid right off.
Richard: I saw a funny film on the tele where a fireman squirted the hose at a man and it knocked him over into some muck.

Six year olds Elizabeth and Ann were washing up in the classroom sink after a cookery session; they were playing with the water as it came from the tap and ran onto the cooking utensils. They regulated the flow of water onto the bowl of a spoon, turning the spoon first one way then another.

Elizabeth: It doesn't drop straight down off the spoon, it spurts out.
Ann: Now turn the spoon round.
Elizabeth: Look it's not going the same way.

They continued their play for approximately ten minutes, using a large and small scoop as well as the spoons.

In addition to these descriptions of children's play that led them to explore the properties of water, teachers recorded many instances of children having mathematical experiences: they counted as they filled and emptied containers; they developed concepts such as volume and shape. No examples are given, since water play has so often been used in this way and teachers are familiar with this aspect.

These examples have been chosen because they are representative of the discoveries that the teachers observed children making for themselves in water play.

1   How water flows: including that it will not flow uphill.
2   That it find its own level.
3   That it takes the shape of its container.
4   That some materials float and some sink in water.
5   That it can be syphoned.
6   That it can be displaced.
7   That it has a resistance.
8   That it exerts pressure.

CLAY

Many teachers observed children playing with clay for the first time. This report is similar to many others in recording the way children find out about the materials:

> Most of the children (a group of girls and boys aged five) started as usual by banging and rolling their clay, using almost everything we provided – rolling-pins, spatulas, and bricks of different shapes and sizes.

The teacher watched some six year olds after giving them clay for the first time in school; they had no tools. Philip took a lump and pressed it with his hands until it was flat. He looked at it for a while and pressed his knuckles into it, making rows of indentations. He regarded these and then flattened them carefully with his thumb. He was silent all the time. The second boy, Richard, picked up his lump and turned it over and over banging it each time, quite gently, on the table. He then stood it upright and pressed hard at each end until he had made a rectangular block. At intervals he said to the others, 'It's coming, look.'

Debbie and Polly made different sized balls rolling them on the table, between their hands and with their fingers. They discussed them, counted them, compared them for size and were concerned that each one should be smooth and round. Bill was much more energetic in his play. He had a heavy lump of clay which he lifted and twisted, throwing it over and over, though in a very controlled way. After wedging it, he stood it on the table and pummelled it with his fists. Then he picked it up and twisted it; finally he announced, 'I'm seeing if I can make a hole right through – I'll have to push hard.'

Bill and Polly and Debbie commented all the time, called on each other to watch and witness the results.

Philip, rolling the clay, said, 'Look I've made a snake – watch if I press it, it gets longer – it's thinner now.'

Five year olds David and Tom were cooperating to make a pre-historic model.

David: It's too hard, we need to wet it, that'll make it soft. (They brought some water.)

Tom: It isn't making it soft, it's slippery now – you feel it.

Rachel and Helen playing alongside discussed clay.

Rachel: This is like Plasticine, it won't roll as thin, it keeps breaking.

Helen: Perhaps it needs water, let's try, I'll get some.

Seven year old Jane, making an octopus, said, 'I must wet the tentacles to stick them on.' Having done this she carefully smoothed over the joins with her finger.

A teacher observed a five year old boy's unsuccessful attempts to give his lambs and chicks legs. She was called away and on her return she asked him where the legs were: he explained, 'They're lying down.'

In contrast a seven year old hunted around until he found a toilet roll carton to 'support the legs' of his dinosaur. A six year old dis-covering that his brontosaurus was too heavy to stand up, squashed it down and made the legs smaller. The problem of balancing his Humpty Dumpty on a wall defeated a five year old, who settled for a hedgehog instead.

Seven year olds Cilla and Pat discussed slip when they were playing.

Cilla: You can make fingerprints with this, watch me.

Pat: I know I'm making them too. It's the wet isn't it.

Cilla: No it's the clay – it isn't the wet 'cos when it dries it's clay – you wait and see – it's coloured.

Pat: I did it before. I thought it was the wet.

Three six year old girls were playing with a set of clay tools. The following dialogue took place.

Joan: With this (a flat tool) I can bang the clay flat and it will make all sorts of shapes – they come out different.

Alice: You're making the same shapes as me.

Joan: I'm not making the same – my patterns aren't the same, 'cos this is different. Look yours isn't the same.

Alice: No, it hasn't got the bit in the middle. (She was using a pronged tool.)

Lisa: I'm nearly making the same but my patterns are going down yours are going across. They're the same 'cos I've left spaces and I've put patterns on top.

What happens to the children in this exploratory play?

1 They enter into conversation.
2 They cooperate.
3 They acquire manipulative skill.
4 They use physical control.
5 They use different tools.
6 They compare and contrast the effects of different tools when used with clay.
7 They improvise in the use of tools or other materials.
8 They compare clay with other materials.
9 They realize that moist clay is pliable and permeable.
10 They realize that dry clay is hard and brittle.
11 They realize that clay only appears to dissolve in water.
12 They realize that weak supports will not hold a heavy superstructure.
13 They realize that superstructure supports must be wider than the model.
14 They realize that angles affect balance.

WOOD

Seven year old George, working with a group of boys, picked up a mallet and examined it carefully, rubbing his finger over it.

George: Look, this end has got all these dents in. You can see the marks of the nails.

Richard: You mustn't use it for nails, must you.

George: It's because it's not hard enough. The nails go in there and you bang them in – that's what the marks are – see, feel them.

(The mallet was passed round the group.)

John: What do you use it for then? I thought it was a hammer.

Richard: I'll ask my dad, he's got one. He said he had it when he used to go camping.

A six year old girl rubbed her finger along a piece of wood. Her friend said, 'Don't. You'll get splinters, you have to rub it with sandpaper to smooth it. Then the bits don't come off in splinters.'

A five year old boy tried unsuccessfully to saw a piece of wood, then he started to hit the wood with the saw.

Lesley: Don't do that. It's not a chopper, it's a saw.

The teacher went over to the group and asked them to look carefully at the saw edge.

Bill: It's like teeth.
Mary: Perhaps it bites the wood.
Teacher: Watch me saw this piece of wood and see if you can find out what's happening.
Philip: I know, little bits come off – it's called sawdust – my dad does lots of sawing.
(The children got on their knees to watch.)
Andrew: You can't saw if the wood's very hard. If it's thin it splits, that bit I was using for my wings split when I tried to knock the nail in.
Mary: It does bite that's why the bits come off.
Teacher: Why can you bite things?
Jane: 'Cos our teeth are sharp?
Teacher: Are the teeth on the saw edge sharp?
Lesley: Yes, I made my finger bleed last week.
Philip: If it's not sharp it won't cut – my dad says it's blunt sometimes.
Teacher: Can you bite very hard things?
Mary: You have to suck some sweets, they're too hard to bite – you might break your teeth.
Teacher: That's right – well which do you think is harder, the saw or the wood?
Bill: The saw's bendy.
Andrew: The wood isn't.
Philip: If the saw goes through wood it must be harder.

The discussion continued for a short while and the children looked at pictures of woodchoppers and axes. They decided that a chopper must be much heavier than a saw and that was why it could 'bite much deeper into the wood'. The teacher compared the size of flakes of wood to sawdust. Mary said she had only heard of snowflakes. The discussion ended in laughter when Bill said, 'Sometimes my mum says *she's* flaked out.'

The children in the group were aged five, six and seven, and could have left the discussion, but all five stayed to the end. All participated in the discussion at some time. The teacher decided that the discussion had gone on long enough.

A five year old girl sawing through a piece of wood was nearly through when she cried out, 'It's going to fall off.' She stopped and waited for it to fall off. When it didn't she continued to saw and said, 'You have to go right to the end.'

Another five year old girl, making a bus, nailed wheels on the side, far away from the bottom edge. The teacher asked her if the bus would move. She tried it and said, 'The wheels are too high up, I'll have to take them out.'

Two six year olds found out why the wheels on their car would not turn.

Graham: They're too tight. They stick to the wood.
Malcolm: You banged the nail too hard.
Graham: Let me look. If the nail's too thick it sticks you see. I've made lots of cars.

A teacher noticed a group of children gathered in the school garden. When she went to find out what was interesting them they explained that they were making a bonfire.

Greg: If you rub a stick it makes fire.
Jo: We've seen it on television. Indians do it.

Three boys were taking their boats they had made to the courtyard to sail in the water trough.

Michael: Bet yours doesn't sail, it's too big.
Colin: 'Course it will, they have big boats, don't they. What about those that carry cars?
Mark: They're not made of wood.
Colin: Well trees float don't they – big branches do.

Michael: Mine will be the best, it's only little and it's got a sail.

Mark: And mine will float for sure – it's very light – you feel it.

Unfortunately for Colin his boat was too large to go in the water trough, he had to take it home and try it in the bath!

Two six year olds, Jim and Angela, were playing with wood. They decided to make models, Angela a bird table and Jim a boat. Angela was using a tenon-saw to cut a length of wood in half; she had made one cut and turned the wood in the vice. She started to saw again. Jim who was more experienced stopped her and pointed out that the cuts would not meet. She either did not understand or did not believe him. The teacher gathered a group of interested children and asked for their advice. It was quickly suggested that you could draw a line so that you would know where you wanted to saw.

David: Like when you cut with scissors.

Jim: If you bang it on your knee won't it break?

Teacher: Can you break wood or do you always have to saw or chop?

Helen: You can break a twig.

Fiona: A twig isn't wood.

Helen: Of course it is.

David: It comes off a tree.

Jim: You can only break it if it's thin – you can't break a great big bit.

Unfortunately the bell for school assembly rang and the discussion ended.

Teachers can now answer these questions:

1 The children asked the teacher to intervene here. What did her intervention achieve?

2 What did the children learn?

3 What more could she have done if the interruption had not occurred?

4 Is it true to say the problem grew in their play, and the children became so involved in it, because they had to solve it to continue their play?

Using Play with Natural Materials

1   Provide as many natural materials as you can to give the children the opportunity to experience sensory, imaginative and exploratory play.

2   Observe all play with each of the materials in turn as often as possible with the intention of participating, initiating, and intervening.

3   Record your objectives and the results of becoming involved.

4   Record the learning and development in the play.

Reference

PIAGET, J. (1961) *Play, Dreams and Imitation in Childhood* Heinemann

8 Play Outdoors

This chapter outlines the reasons why teachers provide Play Outdoors, how it is organized, and the problems that it brings. It covers the four categories of play described in earlier chapters and shows how new dimensions can be given to them outside.

Reasons for providing Play Outdoors

Fresh air

1 Some children have no safe outdoor space near home where they may play. They spend the evenings and weekends watching television or playing indoors.

2 In winter children spend the daylight hours at school. They can therefore only play out of doors during school terms at weekends.

Space

1 The majority of children are restricted at home by lack of space. Most gardens provide limited opportunity for play. Streets are not safe unless they are designated 'Play Streets'.

2 A survey of young children's play (1966) suggests that they prefer to be within calling distance of home. They will not go to play in parks or on commons unless they are taken by older children or adults.

3 One of the most common complaints of the teachers observing play in the Project is lack of space in the classroom. Many comment on the difficulty of finding space for shops, houses and hospitals as described in the Domestic Play chapter. Imaginative play like that described in the 'Cowboys and Indians' situation in the chapter on Make/Believe Play, requires room for vigorous movement as well as large 'props'. It is often inhibited by the activities of the other children, the need to take care not to knock against other children's constructions, painting easels and water troughs.

The playground or other outdoor areas provide room for this energetic play. When some children can remain indoors while others play outside there is obviously more room for the indoor activities as well. Even at playtime, space to play may be confined. To quote one teacher: 'At playtime numbers restrict play. We have over two hundred infants using the playground.'

4 Energetic children are more ready to concentrate on sedentary pursuits when they are given ample opportunity for vigorous play.

5 New entrants to school are accustomed to the free run of the home. If they are confined to a crowded classroom they find the

restriction of their movements very trying. This may affect their
attitude to school and learning.

Noise

1 In school only a low level of noise is acceptable.
2 When young children play, noise is unavoidable. Their voices
   rise when they make some discovery or achieve success. Some
   imaginative situations require accompanying sounds. Wood, sand,
   water, bricks are all at times noisy play materials.
3 Outside noise is permissible. Children can hammer, saw, sandpaper, knock down bricks, scrape along the base of a sand tray,
   blow down tubes, imitate animal or Dalek sounds without disturbing other children or other classes. They are free to use their
   voices and shout excitedly. There are no classroom walls to
   reverberate!
4 Experiments with sound can be encouraged outside. Many schools
   have to restrict or forbid this kind of play indoors because they
   have no place in which it can occur without disturbing other
   children. Individuals or small groups cannot play with sound; it
   either must involve the whole class or be omitted altogether from
   the curriculum.
5 New entrants may include two types of children. One type comes
   from homes such as flats, where the children have never been able
   to make a noise and for this reason are inhibited in their play
   with other children. A second group has never been made aware
   of noise and these children do not know how to control their
   voices when playing. Both groups need a time and place to be
   noisy at school if they are to discover how to control noise or how
   to consider others.

Mess

Despite all the amenities of modern school buildings much infant
play is regulated by the amount of mess that can be easily cleared or
cleaned:

1 Sand and water if spilt on some surfaces indoors can cause
   children to slip. These materials are not as slippery on a playground surface.
2 Floor coverings can be difficult to clean if clay, paint, sand or
   water are dropped. The playground does not have to be cleaned
   nor does the caretaker have to be so understanding!
3 In the classroom the unavoidable proximity of 'messy' play

materials to expensive equipment inhibits their use. There is more space in the playground; precious materials can be kept apart from messy play activities.

Time

1 When play occurs outside it can often be allowed to develop over a period of time that is not possible in the classroom.
2 Space can be used longer as it is not required for other activities.
3 The children are more highly motivated to develop their ideas when they know they will not be suddenly stopped.
4 Mess can be left for longer without inconveniencing others.
5 Noise can be allowed to continue without disturbing other children.
6 Children new to school are given time to adjust and do not have to be constantly changing their activities.

Adjustment to school

1 Nursery and reception class teachers recognize the new entrant who is reluctant to be parted from his hat and coat, and they provide the opportunity for playing outdoors where he does not need to take them off.
2 Playing outdoors is a familiar occupation; many new entrants are encouraged to feel secure at school through long periods of outdoor play.
3 Even older children who have adjusted to school may be helped to overcome temporary emotional problems by the feeling of freedom that accompanies outdoor play.
4 At times children need to be alone or a group needs a private place to play, which may be impossible to cater for in a crowded classroom and school. Playing outdoors gives children the opportunity to be separate from the class.
5 Children who are frightened of 'playtime' in mid-morning or at dinner time may be helped to become familiar with the large playground while playing with children whom they know, and when accompanied by their own teacher.

Discovering the outside environment

1 New materials can be found. Soil and clay can be moulded and dug, they react quite differently from the sand and clay provided in school. Leaves, wild flowers, twigs, seeds, pebbles, stones can be used for imaginative play.
2 Climbing materials are different: there are trees, logs, concrete blocks, stepping stones, shapes and mazes.

3   Wind dries sand which then blows in the wind; the wind changes direction, so does the moving sand.

4   Water is affected by the wind; the surface moves, it flows differently on windy days as you pour it.

5   Washing from domestic play dries in the wind. Some children only have experience of the spin drier at home and in the launderette.

6   Sometimes the wind is strong enough to blow down a tower or wall of building bricks. The higher the tower the more easily it is blown down.

7   The wind blows balls, hoops, skittles, skipping ropes; in a strong wind they are uncontrollable.

8   Sun dries the sand in the outside pit. It also dries the washing.

9   Paint and paste dry and harden in the sun. Clay becomes dry in the hot sun and difficult to mould.

10   Feet make imprints in the sand pit; wet feet make footprints on the ground when you leave the paddling pool; they disappear quickly if the sun is out or the ground warm.

11   Rain sounds different as it falls on different surfaces. Raindrops make patterns in dry and damp sand, in puddles and in the paddling pool.

12   Temperature – warm water in the water trough usually gets colder more quickly outside than in the classroom.

13   Light and shade – the sky and clouds are noticed in play outside.

14   Light changes; paintings look different in the sunlight; gaudy dressing-up clothes appear drab in the shade. Shadows are not always to be seen; they change and move.

15   Perception changes outdoors. Children think they can throw a ball a long way in the hall because it reaches the far wall. In the playground the same throw does not seem to send the ball very far. A tower of twelve bricks looks high in a classroom, outside it is dwarfed by the height of the school building.

16   In the paddling or swimming pool children's perception of water is quite different from that gained by leaning over a sink or water trough.

17   Outside there may be sufficient sand to walk and kneel in; children feel it with their feet and knees as well as their hands. The perspective is different.

18   The playground smells different after rain. Clothes dried outside smell different from those dried in the classroom. The grass smells after the lawn has been cut. Petrol fumes from cars can be smelled in the playground.

19 Voices sound different outside. Sometimes they are louder, sometimes harder to hear, sometimes they are distorted, sometimes they echo.

Organization of Play Outdoors

Play outdoors is successful and enjoyed by teachers and children when:

1 it is very carefully organized by the teachers
2 the children thoroughly understand the organization
3 it takes place as regularly as weather permits.

These three points are developed below.

1 *Organization involved*

   (a) Liaison with other members of staff to share supervision, to make sure that the removal of equipment outside does not inconvenience anyone; to allocate playground time; to agree about the time and place acceptable for noise.

   (b) A ruling about which play activities will take place outside. This is necessary, whether all the children or only groups go outdoors.

   (c) Allocating definite areas of the outdoor play space to certain activities and equipment.

   (d) Arranging the order and manner in which equipment and materials are carried out and back.

   (e) Ensuring that, at clearing-up time, the children who have brought their equipment in know what they are to do while the remainder are still engaged in the removal.

   (f) Allowing sufficient time for carrying equipment in and out.

2 *The children's tasks*

   (a) The rules about carrying equipment and materials must be clear and simple enough for the children to understand and obey.

   (b) The order in which equipment is carried out and in must be arranged and strictly adhered to.

   (c) All the children should know how to carry all the equipment, and where it is to be placed outdoors.

   (d) Individual children may have specific tasks but any child should be able to stand in for another, or to assist when difficulties arise.

(e) The organization of outdoor play must be known to all the children, e.g. that play with ropes takes place within a specified area.

(f) Periodically the children should be consulted and the rules and organization reviewed in the light of their suggestions.

3 *Frequency*

(a) The carrying in and out of equipment will become easier and quicker every time it happens.

(b) Children are not excited by the novelty of being outside when it is a regular event.

(c) Passers-by cease to be amazed when they are accustomed to seeing play outdoors.

(d) Junior and middle school children are less likely to be distracted by a daily occurrence.

(e) Parents accept outdoor play as part of the school curriculum when it is the custom.

(f) Children are more likely to adapt their play to the advantages of being outside when they have time to be aware of the possibilities of the environment.

Provision for Play Outdoors

Teachers will select from this comprehensive list of play activities to suit the number of children playing outside, the circumstances controlling the removal of materials and equipment outside, and the children's play interests at any given time.

1 Water, sand, wood and clay can be taken outside. They are usually considered to be the messiest and noisiest play activities likely to cause most damage to floor coverings inside.

2 If the indoor sand tray has no wheels and cannot be moved outside, there is the possibility of providing sand on the ground, in a confined area as described earlier.

3 Carrying water to fill the water trough outside is a task requiring skill and practice in capacity and weight and therefore useful to the children. Receptacles for carrying water and sand must be available.

4 Clay can be moulded on low walls or on polythene sheets on the ground. The children will still wear the all-enveloping shirts from home or the overalls provided by school. If necessary, a jug of water and bowl can be available for washing hands before

the children return to the classroom.

5 Some dressing-up materials can be kept especially for play indoors if the teacher finds that the more delicate or pale-coloured materials are unsuited to outdoors.

6 Lack of space indoors may mean that energetic play, for example, Indians, space rockets, monsters, can only take place outside. 'Props' for these are therefore only provided for play outdoors.

7 Blankets or rugs may be kept for play outdoors and used to throw over logs or climbing frames to make tree houses or cowboy look-outs.

8 Large cardboard boxes (e.g. deep-freeze, television cabinets, washing machine containers) that take up too much room inside are especially suited to large construction play outdoors. If children wish to paint them, floor coverings do not have to be considered.

9 Full-scale models which the children make and want to play with are often too large for play inside. A Dalek, a dragon or a dinosaur are dwarfs in the playground.

10 Bird tables and bookshelves can be hammered on the ground outside; when large pieces of wood are obtained, they can be kept for outdoor play.

11 Houses with several rooms, cowboy forts with watch towers or castellated castles can be built with large blocks, boxes and planks in the spacious playground.

12 Domestic play can take the form of picnics, markets, excursions to the park, perambulations with baby, hanging out the washing. It may not require all the 'house furniture' that is used in the classroom.

13 Painting easels can be carried out; this gives good practice in balance. Most schools are provided with non-spill paint pots.

14 If small collage or scrap models are to be provided for, a polythene groundsheet may serve instead of tables and chairs. A bucket of water can stand outside to wash paste brushes if necessary.

15 Lego and other small play materials can also be used on mats as they often are in the classroom.

16 Railway layouts and motorways, aerodromes, boats and model harbours can be extensive, and therefore imaginative in a new way in the playground.

17 Mats enable children who are not playing to sit or sprawl and read.

18 A few chairs and a table provide for those who are writing.

19   Play with balls, hoops, ropes, skittles may not be possible if the space is not large enough for them to be relegated to one area. Jumping stands, climbing frames, stilts, balancing bars, stepping stones and physical play that young children can control may be the most energetic form of play that can be allowed. An area of the outside playground can be set aside for such play.

Play dependent on space

Rubber tyres

Darren and Philip aged six were playing with rubber tyres, bouncing in them and moving about the playground. 'We're in boats,' they cried, and when they fell out, 'Oh, we're in the sea, we're drowning. Swim, quick, swim to the boats, climb back in.'

Robert the Bruce

Joanne aged seven joined six boys to play Robert the Bruce. They had been reading the story in a Ladybird book. They discussed at length the kind of weapons needed and decided on spears, bows and arrows, and rifles. When they had manufactured their imaginary weapons they acted the story. Joanne wanted to observe a spider to discover how a web was spun, but the spider was 'uncooperative' so she withdrew from the group, found a book on spiders and consulted the pictures. She used wool to make her web. When the other children were dissatisfied with particular scenes they repeated them, especially the battle scene! Arguments occurred when a child did not want to be taken prisoner, but were resolved without adult intervention. The children were still engrossed after an hour's play and were eager to repeat the story. The most timid boy in the group became so involved in his role that he played aggressively and dramatically. Throughout the game the leader remained unchallenged.

'Junk-men'

Daniel, Michael and Peter, aged seven, were playing together in the playground. Daniel, pulling a wheelbarrow, had a rope tied round his waist as reins. Michael was sitting in the wheelbarrow holding a whip he had made from a stick and a skipping rope.

Michael: Come on, let's go to Golder's Hill Park to collect the junk.

He cracked the whip and Daniel galloped off to the brick box where

168

Peter was stationed. Peter helped Michael to load the wheelbarrow with bricks and then hitched himself side by side with Daniel to the wheelbarrow.

Daniel: Good, we got it loaded up now with flat pieces.
Michael: Grr-up horses.

He cracked the whip again. They galloped to the far corner of the playground where they removed the bricks from the barrow and laid them carefully on the ground in a tessellated pattern to make a pavement.

Daniel: You've been the man all the time. Oh, all right, I'll be the horse again.

As Michael sat in the barrow, Daniel hitched himself up and they trotted off, leaving Peter laying the pavement. They galloped to a 'camp' which another group of seven year olds had made from trestles and mats, and left abandoned.

Daniel: Michael we're *all* men and this is our house.

The two boys returned a number of times with barrow loads of bricks for Peter to lay. On one journey Daniel carried bricks in his hands.

Daniel: Come on Michael, you're not helping.

Michael was fixing his rope to the stick as his whip had come adrift. He went to help Peter.

Michael: It's all right, I've got a new horse now.

Nerendhra, a newcomer to the play, was wearing the reins and Daniel at last was the 'man' in the wheelbarrow!

Picnics
House play outdoors often takes the form of picnics. Even when there is a Wendy house structure outside, the children remove the domestic play equipment, even the cooker, on to the grass and announce, 'We're having a picnic'. A group of rising-fives first built a caravan with the community blocks and set up a picnic, announcing

that they were by the river. When the picnic was over the boys moved in on their own and converted the caravan into a hideout, complete with roof.

Feeding the lions
When climbing frames are used in play outdoors, the imaginative situations developed can encompass larger areas than is allowed when a whole class has PE in a hall.

Six boys and three girls from a reception class played one morning on the climbing frame. At first it was a cage and the children were lions. They were fed with 'meat'.

Andrew: Let's use the red ones – they're more like meat. (He was feeding the lions with pieces of Lego.)
Paul: Quick, one's getting away – catch it, run after it.
Andrew: If you feed them they won't chase you – they'll stay in the cage.

Later the climbing frame became a boat.

Andrew: Come on – the boat's going to Africa.
Warren: Yeah – come on we're taking the lions home. No, you can't come on the ship.
Ann: Why? I'm playing with you – I'm one of the lions.
Andrew: You don't get girls on ships.
Elizabeth: Why not?
Paul: You just don't that's all.

A little later the climbing frame was a rocket.

Andrew: We're going to Mars – there are monsters on Mars.
Warren: Yeah, we'll have to make some ray-guns.
Paul: Come on we'll make them over here.

They spent a long time manufacturing ray-guns with Lego and eventually overcame the problem of making them portable. They then fought the monsters after the rocket landed. Their teacher commented: 'The group was very fluid – boys leaving to see caterpillars and then rejoining the play – with all the space available, nobody seemed to mind who came and went.'

Firemen
Jonathan and Marcus, aged five, hooked two planks on to the climb-

ing frame and, dressed in jackets and hats, pretended to be firemen putting out a fire. Jonathan had the fireman's helmet because he was the chief and Marcus wore the peaked cap. The planks were firemen's ladders.

Jonathan: Hurry – you climb up that ladder. Marcus – catch this – it's to put the water in. (He picked up a length of rope and used it like a hose.) No – I know – you stay down there – go back – go down – that's right – now you turn the water on.
Marcus: I'm turning it on now – the water's coming.
Jonathan: Melissa – we're firemen – we're coming to put the fire out. Pretend you're in the flats. (Melissa was already on the climbing frame.)
Melissa: Yeah – you've got to rescue me – I'm coming down here now – I'm coming down this ladder.
Jonathan: Marcus, you catch her at the bottom.
Marcus: OK. You look after the water. I'm coming to help you now – I'm climbing up this ladder.

In this play outdoors where the children took full advantage of the extra space available, they were:

1 cooperating in group play
2 practising physical skills
3 engaging in role play
4 using language to direct the play, maintain their position, imagine, predict and project
5 solving problems that occurred in the course of the play
6 improvising in their use of materials
7 being motivated to recall the correct order of events
8 being motivated to refer to books and pictures and observe accurately.

Noisy play

Tarzan
Three six year old boys and a girl were playing together on the climbing frame.

Stephen: Aw-wa-ooh – Aw-wa-ooh – I'm Tarzan – I'm coming to rescue you.

Susan:	I'm Jane – I'm up here in our tree house. Aw-wa-ooh.
Keith:	You can't make that noise – that's Tarzan's call.
Susan:	It's Jane's call too – see – you don't know, I call Tarzan when I want to be rescued. I'm letting him know his dinner's ready. Who are you then?
Keith:	I'm Cheetah. (He jumped up and down on his bar and made a chattering noise.)
Colin:	I'm Boy – I live with Tarzan too. So I can call Aw-wa-ooh.
Stephen:	Look I've got this tyre – I know – let's tie it on here so we can swing on it.
Susan:	You do that while I finish getting the dinner – I've got to go into the jungle to get more bananas. Cheetah you come with me.
Keith:	OK.
Colin:	Tarzan I'm helping you – throw the rope up to me – I'm good at doing knots.

The play continued for twenty minutes with all four using the tyre to swing from the climbing frame to the ground. Sometimes they pretended to fight wild animals and Cheetah jumped up and down applauding. Stones and leaves were collected by Susan for their meal, and arranged picnic-style on the ground when she found it impossible to balance them on bars. Tarzan's call was repeated many times and often echoed by other children playing elsewhere.

Monsters
John and Michael, two six year olds, were hiding behind a bush and emerging as monsters every time the girls walked by with their prams. Each time the girls screamed and ran away only to pass that way again when the monsters had returned to their den. The teacher intervened to explain that the calls for help were disturbing other children, and asked how they could prevent this.

Jennifer:	(She was the mother in the house play.) Let's pretend they are friendly monsters and we ask them home for a meal.
John:	Yeah – you get a monster meal ready for us – we'll eat ever such a lot – sausages.
Michael:	I won't. I'm only a baby monster – I don't hurt anybody – I'm a kind monster.
John:	You call us when you're ready – we're going to find some other friendly monsters.

The girls then prepared a meal and the monsters collected two other boys to join them in the monsters' den. They brought lengths of material from the dressing-up clothes, and boxes from the junk collection. With these they made themselves into monsters and caused much laughter when they tried to eat their meal in the house. When the boys became kind monsters they walked about making low growling noises; the girls now took them by the hand and walked along with them or went to hold conversations with them about their food.

A circus

Mandy and Louise, aged seven, organized a circus. They started when Mandy held a tyre for Louise to jump through.

Louise: It's like the circus on the television. I'm a poodle doing tricks.

Mandy: I'll shout out 'Hup-la' like the man and you jump.

Louise: Right – wait 'til I'm ready. No, just a minute – don't shout yet. Sarah, come on, you can be in the circus, get some more. You three get the tyres and we'll be dogs.

Mandy: Yes – when I shout you all jump. I'll say one, two, three, jump.

Louise: When we've jumped in the tyres – pretend they're like hoops with paper in – you all follow me along this plank and back again. All you others watch and shout and clap when we've finished.

Mandy: Hurry up and get ready then – it's hard holding these tyres like this.

Louise: Watch me how I climb through and walk along the plank on my two back legs.

Gradually a group of children collected to watch and Mandy organized them in a circle ''cos they have a ring in a circus' and developed other tricks for the 'dogs' to perform, using balls and skittles.

Moon rocket

A group of five and six year olds were playing on the climbing frame. They imagined it was a rocket going to the moon. Three other children asked if they could go to the moon. Julie decided to stay on earth when she discovered that her scooter was too big to go in the rocket. Her two companions were allowed to take their run-abouts because they could be 'moon buggies'. The astronauts counted down to zero and blasted off. When they landed on the moon they collected 'gold nuggets' in a wheelbarrow and brought them back to the rocket which then returned to earth. The teacher accompanied them on their next trip and it was decided that she should be the queen, not an astronaut. On this trip the rocket was attacked and the children made shooting noises at each other.

Mountaineering

A group of boys of mixed ages tied ropes on to the climbing frame and played at mountaineering. The teacher checked and was surprised to find the knots quite safe. The boys then began to climb the frame, using the ropes and calling to each other as they climbed. Later they discussed with the teacher how mountaineers fastened their ropes on a mountainside, and what kind of equipment and training they needed. Later still the mountaineers became cowboys; they used their ropes as lassoes and the climbing frame as horses. Once again they 'hallooed' and called to each other as they caught their imaginary steers.

During this noisy play outdoors the children were:

1 cooperating in groups
2 engaging in role play
3 developing their understanding of language
4 solving problems
5 practising physical skills
6 recalling television and films
7 improvising in the use of materials.

Play using the outdoor environment and equipment

Some play is only possible outdoors since it is inspired by the environment or the outdoor equipment.

'Hoop-la'

A group of children from a vertically grouped class were playing house with cups and saucers and plates. One discovered that the wind carried a plastic saucer when he tossed it to his companion. The others were intrigued and all practised throwing the plates and saucers. They decided to abandon the domestic play and develop a fair and 'hoop-la' stall. The teacher intervened to compare the flight of the plates with other shapes and objects.

Hot surfaces

Some rising-fives playing on a slide complained that it was so hot it was burning them. Their teacher turned it round so that the slide was away from the sun. The children noticed how quickly it cooled and how they could use it again. After talking with the teacher, some of the group went round feeling the cars parked in the playground and returned with the news that the white car was the coolest.

Bubbles

Another group in the same playground were blowing bubbles with long lengths of plastic tube. Some boys ran about trying to catch the bubbles in bottles; when one succeeded he cried out, 'Look it's like a cork'. They compared the sizes of the bubbles and how far they floated before they broke. Finally, they noticed the colours and talked about similar sets of colour, mentioning a rainbow and petrol on the road.

In the chapter on Natural Materials there is also a description of outside play with bubbles.

The figurehead

In a playground that contained a punt, a log cabin and several logs for climbing on, a teacher observed some six year olds playing in the boat which had proper oars. Two boys were rowing and Maria was standing at the front with her arms outstretched.

Maria: I'm the figurehead.
Nigel: There's a storm coming, row hard.
Linda: I'll be on the lookout. (She stood high on the back of the boat.)
Jeremy: We're the Loch Ness monsters. (He and Jason tried to climb into the boat.)
Nigel: You can't get in – monsters don't get into boats.
    (The children in the boat pushed the monsters away.)
David: There's a hole here – I've got my foot over it – quick bale the water out.
    (They all pretended to bale the water out.)
Nigel: Land ahead – all off – we're on land now.
Linda: Yes – we're at Treasure Island.

Jeremy carefully lifted Maria (the figurehead) off and put her on dry land. The boys then went off to find the treasure and brought some wooden boxes back to the boat. Linda brought the 'figurehead' back to the boat.

Linda:	A monster had got her. I'll put her back. (She placed Maria back in the boat.)
Maria:	Change places – you be the figurehead now.
Nigel:	We're going to bury the treasure now 'cos we're smugglers.
David:	Quick, get in the boat, the monsters are grabbing us.

As the smugglers fought the monsters, the girls seized their opportunity to use the oars and started to row. Jeremy and Jason stole the treasure and hid it in the log cabin.

Nigel:	I'm keeping watch for other ships. (He stood with his hand to his eyes, looking out.)
Maria:	Our arms are aching, we can't row much more.
David:	We can put up the sails.
Nigel:	Yeah it's windy – you can stop rowing now. We're putting the sails up.
	(Maria returned to her position as figurehead.)

The group then broke up, the girls to play house and the boys to build a prison with road blocks. The play had lasted for twenty minutes and two boys wrote a story about it later.

The teacher who observed and described the play added a note that 'during the previous week, the class had visited Greenwich to see the Cutty Sark and the Maritime Museum'.

Robbers

A group of seven year old boys used a hut in another outside play space as a bank. Robbers climbed in through a 'broken window' and carried out pretend bags of money.

At the same time a second group had converted the nearby lookout tower into a cavalry post. They carried up large pieces of wood to serve as cannons but the battlemented top hindered their movement. 'Still there's enough room to move them a little bit,' Stephen explained. The space under the lookout was used as a dungeon and the captives were imprisoned there. 'From the lookout you can see a long way – you can see the top of the climbing frame.'

Boats

In the same outdoor play space, on another occasion, the children made a boat out of a wooden frame, using planks as seats and poles as oars. They later added a sail. When the oars disturbed other children playing near, the teacher suggested the boat should become a punt. The insects that were uncovered when a plank was moved from the grass, to be used for a pole, caused great interest and much conversation.

If these examples are examined carefully it is obvious that the children gained all the experiences that have been described in space and noisy play. But it is also obvious that the outdoor environment enables children to be observant and make scientific discoveries in a way that is not possible indoors.

Teachers can now work out for themselves, using the examples in which a teacher was involved:

1   why she was involved
2   what form her involvement took
3   what was the result
4   could she have been involved in any other way.

Similarly, analyse the examples in which there is no teacher involved, and decide:

1   whether an adult could have been involved
2   what form her involvement could have taken
3   what would have been the result.

Problems of Play Outdoors

It may be that the difficulties some schools would have to contend with are too great to enable them to provide outdoor play, despite its advantages. It is unfortunately most probable that schools with the greatest difficulties are often in areas where children are not able to play out of doors at home, i.e. where there is the greatest need for the provision of outdoor play in school time. Yet some SPA schools are generously staffed with welfare assistants, and in this respect may be better able to supervise play out of doors, and the carrying in and out of equipment.

We can only suggest that teachers weigh the advantages and disadvantages of providing outdoor play in their school, taking into account the home environment of the children and the opportunities given to them to enjoy fresh air, move in space, and be noisy.

Providing the opportunity for infants to play out of doors always brings problems. Here are some reported by teachers who worked on the Project.

1 Neither teachers nor welfare assistants nor caretakers have sufficient time to carry in and out all the necessary materials and equipment for play outside.
2 In some schools, materials and equipment need to be carried through a hall, along corridors and up and down stairs.
3 Sometimes it is necessary to pass through another classroom.
4 Doors are often narrow and heavy to prop open.
5 Playgrounds adjoin busy roads.
6 Middle or junior school classes complain about distractions.
7 Many schools have no outside sand pits or paddling pools. Some that have must contend with vandals and unwelcome canine or feline visitors. Covers that are provided are so heavy and unwieldy that even the most cooperative caretaker is daunted.
8 Materials and equipment deteriorate more quickly when they are carried in and out.
9 Where outside access is not easy, it is necessary to have the whole class outside. This may prevent other classes from using the playground.
10 When the school has a 'playtime', materials and equipment will have to be removed. This will limit the time for play outdoors.
11 Even in schools where outside access is easy, the teachers often have difficulty in supervising children indoors and outdoors.
12 Time is wasted carrying materials and equipment outside.
13 Parents remember their own schooldays and complain that children are not being educated unless they are 'in school'.
14 School activities are on view in the playground and play must be justified to the viewers.
15 The weather is seldom suited to outdoor play – we live in the wrong climate. Playgrounds are badly sited for wind and sun.
16 Sudden changes in the weather have to be catered for.
17 Playground surfaces spoil mats and other floor coverings.

Looking for solutions
How far do the following suggestions help to solve these problems? (The numbers correspond to the problems listed above.)

1 All materials and equipment used outside are carried by the children.

2 Equipment that is too heavy or unwieldy for the children to transport is left indoors; other improvised equipment and materials are used instead, or play with these is restricted to indoors. Teachers and welfare assistants help at times but the children must be able to manage without adult assistance.

3 There are three possibilities when outside access is only obtained through another classroom:

(a) The two teachers concerned agree to combine their classes for the outdoor play sessions and both go out.

(b) The classes are combined but one teacher remains indoors with half the children, and the other stays outdoors with the children who go out.

(c) The teachers organize their day so that the class going out is able to carry equipment through when the other class has vacated the room, e.g. during a hall period. Equipment is carried back at lunch time or 'playtime'.

4 Heavy doors are fixed with a catch and bar that fastens them back until all the equipment has been carried through. Equipment that is too wide, even when up-ended or manoeuvred sideways to pass through narrow doorways, must remain inside.

5 If the noise of traffic is troublesome, the outdoor space is organized so that noisy play (e.g. carpentry) and play that does not involve much dialogue (e.g. painting) takes place near to the road.

6 When infants use the playground frequently, junior and middle school children grow accustomed to them; the novelty wears off and they are less likely to be distracted. The equipment can be organized so that the least disturbing play takes place near to the classrooms. Infant and junior or first and middle schools can cooperate and match their programmes so that noisier active sessions for the older children coincide with the outdoor play sessions of the younger.

7 (a) Sand and water trays can be transported outside if they are on wheels.

(b) If the trays are immovable, plastic bowls and baths are specially provided and are filled and emptied in the playground.

(c) Schools that want children to have large outdoor sand areas enclose a polythene sheet with walls of bricks and put sand inside.

(d) Parents are often willing to construct practical covers for outdoor sand pits and paddling pools.

8   Schools that provide for frequent play outdoors use an outdoor store for some of their play equipment. Frequently this is purchased by the PTA or with funds raised by parents and teachers specifically for this purpose. If vandalism is a problem in the area, schools reduce outdoor play equipment to a minimum and store it inside.

9   If more than one class wishes to use a small playground for play outdoors, there are two possible solutions:
   (a) They share the equipment and the time, the first class carrying it out and leaving it for the last class to carry back.
   (b) Two or more classes combine; one teacher remains indoors and one outdoors.

10 When schools are providing the opportunity of play outdoors for all their children, they re-examine the need for 'playtime'. Why did schools institute playtime?

   (a) To give children fresh air.
   (b) To give children the chance to be physically active.
   (c) To give children the chance to talk and be noisy.
   (d) To give children the chance to go to the lavatory.
   (e) To give children relaxation from the concentrated effort required by learning.
   (f) To give children the chance to play together.
   (g) To give teachers a respite from children.
   (h) To give children a respite from teachers.
   (i) To give teachers a chance to smoke.
   (j) To give teachers a chance to have a cup of coffee or tea.
   (k) To give teachers and monitors the chance to set out materials for the next lesson.

   How many of these reasons hold good for today's infant/first schools?
   How many are fulfilled by play outdoors?
   Many schools no longer have playtime in the afternoon; not as many have dispensed with the morning playtime.
   Can teachers still have coffee if children have no playtime, or can they have their coffee without leaving the children or organize a rota to allow teachers a 'break' in turn?
   Do we need to remind ourselves that 'playtime' was instituted before children had school dinners and a long session in the playground at lunchtime?
   Do we need to ask why many children find excuses to 'stay in' at playtime?

11 If teachers are unable to supervise two groups of children, one in and one out, they must stipulate that the whole class will participate in outdoor play. This means as wide a range of activities as possible is provided and that the whole class is available for transporting equipment and materials.

12 The carrying of equipment and materials by children is not a waste of school time since they learn to organize and to be responsible for equipment.

13 Many infant and first schools encourage parents to come to school to join in school activities. In this way parents learn about new ways of teaching and learning, and understand the purpose of play in school.

14 PTA and other meetings with parents can be arranged to explain the reasons for providing play outdoors.

15 Before they come to school, most children spend much of their day outside. Nursery schools find there are comparatively few days in the school year when children are unable to play outside. Children can wear outdoor clothes for playing outdoors in cold weather.

16 With regular outdoor play sessions and the consequent practice in carrying equipment, children become adept and can move the materials quite quickly. Where outside access is easy, some teachers may not mind moving in and out more than once on showery days. Teachers who have difficult 'journeys' are more likely to stay in once they have returned.

   The majority of teachers on the Project had classrooms with easy access to the outside.

17 Ground coverings can be kept for play outdoors. Jumble sales or appeals to parents often help to solve this problem. If several ground coverings are available, many children can play on the ground and this means less furniture has to be removed.

18 'Cooperative' or 'team' teaching helps to overcome many of the difficulties of providing outdoor play.

Teachers' tasks in Play Outdoors
If a teacher has decided that the children in her class will gain from sessions of play outdoors, she will need to answer these questions:

1 Does the whole class have to be out, or is it possible to have some children in and some out?
2 What kind of play outdoors is to be provided?

3 How is play outdoors different in its requirements from play inside?
4 What kind of equipment and materials will be needed outside?
5 Can the children be shown how to carry all this equipment and all these materials out?
6 How can the children improvise outdoors to compensate for equipment that cannot be transported?
7 What kind of outdoor environment is available?
8 How can I ensure that the children utilize it to the full?
9 How will other classes be affected? What compromises or agreements must be reached with other staff?
10 How often, weather permitting, can outdoor play be provided – every day, every other day, all day, half a day, half a morning, half an afternoon?

Using Play Outdoors
1 Take outside as often as possible the four categories of play described previously.
2 Let the children play in the outside environment using the outside resources such as banks, wind, and the special outside equipment.
3 Observe all the play and record the learning and development.
4 Try to incorporate the special outdoor experiences in the classroom activities.

Reference
NATIONAL BUILDING SOCIETIES (1966) Research Paper 39 *Children's Play on Housing Estates* HMSO

PART 3

The teacher and play

9 Organizational problems

The problems specific to the different categories of play, e.g. the provision of water where there is no tap in the classroom, making house furniture where none is provided or moving equipment for play outside, have been discussed in Part 2. Some suggestions were also given to overcome the problems of space, time and noise.

However, teachers working in the Project highlighted three organizational problems when providing for play in the infant school programme:

1 how to fit play into the curriculum
2 how to clear up play
3 how to record play.

We now look at each of these in turn.

Fitting play into the curriculum

Parts 1 and 2 have shown that if play is to be a learning process it must be structured. This is true however much time is allocated to play in the infant school programme, whether the children are allowed to play all day, half a day or twice a week. It has become clear that many schools only allow play for short periods because, although they agree that children learn and develop through play and that play is a motivating force for learning and development, they find the organizational problem difficult to solve. The problem is concerned with fitting in all the activities that occur in an infant classroom. It relates not only to play but to the whole infant curriculum. Attempts to solve this problem reflect the way in which a school marries circumstances and philosophy. It is not our task, even if it were possible, to prescribe one type of organization. The basic question, 'Where do I fit play into my classroom organization?' has to be answered by each individual teacher and depends on her own situation and her own ideas.

In Appendix 2 we suggest some books on organization which teachers may find helpful to read when considering the total organization of their class.

Clearing up play

Clearing up is an essential part of play in the classroom, although different kinds of play materials may require different sorts of organization and raise different problems. It is, however, part of the total structuring of play and each teacher will need to work out how it fits into the pattern of play in her classroom. The points made here apply to all the categories of play.

Clearing up is as important as all the play with the materials, and therefore should not be hurried nor always left to the same children. It is an obvious temptation for a teacher to let the children who are good or quick at putting away do the job, but if we consider all that is involved in clearing away, we realize how many children are being deprived of valuable experience.

Children have to cooperate when they are storing or tidying materials. Sometimes they have to give or accept orders; they have to persevere and discipline themselves to complete what is to many an unfamiliar and unpleasant chore. Some materials can only be stored in a certain way: some may need to be matched for colour, or counted so many to a box. Others may have to be fitted on fixtures or in containers, which demands a degree of manipulative skill. If all the children at different times are employed, it means they all know where and how the materials are kept, so that they can always find them when they need them for play. Order of this kind is vital to successful play in a classroom or school.

It is true that much infant play looks 'messy', but this background of order is what promotes constructive, imaginative, creative play. Materials that are haphazardly stored, incomplete or tattered, lead to disorderly, destructive, shortlived and unproductive play. Children need complete, unbroken, attractive, clean materials and tools if they are to be inspired, and they need to know where to go to find materials quickly, so that they are not frustrated. They also need to be able to store things easily, quickly and methodically if they are expected to tidy up after their play is completed. Clearing up can also mean leaving a construction for next time, or even putting it on display.

All of this takes time and careful organization. The adults can easily be tempted to do much of this work themselves, rather than allowing it to be carried through by the children. This happens more often where the teacher has parents or aides to assist her. Getting out, storing away and clearing up should be learning experiences for the children, not jobs for the adults. Therefore time must be allowed and the children must feel that these tasks are valued and important. It means that much thought needs to be given, not only to the most suitable way of storing (a teacher may have to try several different places and methods to suit her room and space), but also to the organizing of the children.

Some materials can only be stored in a certain way, and must be within reach.

Young children cannot be expected to work out for themselves the overall plan for a play space. Only the adult can organize how many children are needed to move furniture, to empty water containers, to wash cooking utensils and to store construction materials. Children need to be initiated into the methods to be adopted, given long enough to practise and sufficient explanation, guidance and assistance before it can be taken for granted that they can put away unsupervised. Even then they will need periodic reminders, refresher times, and constant praise and encouragement. We are quick enough to grumble if play materials are left untidy or lost, but very often forget to praise when order is maintained.

A problem often encountered in clearing up materials is that different jobs take different lengths of time. What are the children to do who have completed their clearing away, while the time-consuming tasks are still being done? Even if children start clearing away the more difficult materials early, some will finish before others. Unnecessary problems are avoided if the children's next occupation is not one that involves the complete group or class starting at the same time. It is bad planning if, for example, all the children are required to change rooms immediately following tidying away or to listen to a story that obviously must start for all at the same time. Their programme should be arranged so that they can proceed to their next activities individually or in small groups as their tasks are completed. Children are only tempted to hurry a tidying task or leave it uncompleted if they know that they are missing some more interesting or 'teacher-valued' activity. The children need sufficient warning of the approach of clearing-up time. They need to know how long they have left for the immediate playing time, and to be confident that unfinished play can be continued later. This is valuable experience in developing a concept of time, and in cognitive development in organizing ideas to fit into the time.

These are general points that apply to all play situations. It is impossible to describe an ideal storage system for everyone because classrooms and schools, cupboards, stockrooms, drawers, corridors, halls and storage spaces vary so much. We can only suggest that teachers spend time trying out different ways until they have found the most practical for their own situation. Many teachers have discussed their problems with the children, who sometimes make surprisingly practical suggestions.

We know that teachers may find they have to justify time spent in getting out, putting away and caring for play equipment, both to themselves and to parents; we add some reminders of the values already mentioned; there are others teachers will discover for themselves.

1 The social value of cooperating with other children.
2 The social value of organizing a group of one's peers.
3 The social value of being organized by one's peers.
4 The social value of being responsible for tools and equipment one has used oneself.
5 The social discipline of having to clear one's own tools and equipment.
6 The social value of caring for public property.

7 The value of having to persevere until a task is completed.
8 The value of having to persevere at a boring task that is socially necessary as well as to one's own ultimate advantage.
9 The counting involved.
10 The ordering and sorting involved.
11 The measuring involved.
12 The matching involved of colour and shape.
13 The manipulative skill involved.
14 The physical skill involved.
15 The aesthetic pleasure of cleanliness and order.
16 The reading involved in understanding written instructions.
17 The awareness of order when a job is completed.
18 The sense of achievement or success when a task is completed.

Recording play

Recording play is essential if teachers want to develop its potential as a learning process in the classroom. It is important to build up a picture of the play over a period of time in order to develop and structure successfully. Teachers on the Project were asked to record the different categories of play. Records of individual children which teachers keep will naturally include descriptions of the children's play activities. But individual children's records do not provide the detailed information of play that enables teachers to structure play in their classrooms.

Teachers might find it useful to ask themselves the following questions: Why do I record play? What do I record about play? When do I record play? How do I record play? and use this format as a basis for recording the play in their classroom.

Why do I record play?
1 In order to remind me of what has occurred over a period of time.
2 To identify the learning and development.
3 To supplement the profiles of individual children.
4 To enable me to decide how to use space, time, materials and rules that promote play.
5 To see what alterations need to be made with regard to all of these (in 4).
6 To discover why an adult is involved.
7 To discover how often an adult is involved.
8 To discover whether the involvement is always the same.
9 To discover whether the adult's involvement achieves its objectives.

10 To discover how to incorporate the children's play interests in the other classroom activities and how to introduce the other activities into their play.

What do I record?
1 A specific kind of play, i.e. domestic, construction, natural materials, make/believe, outdoor.
2 The date, the length of time, and time of day of the recording.
3 Provision:
Space
(a) Whether any area is used more frequently than others.
(b) Whether the children are using all the space allocated.
(c) Whether the children are trying to find more space.
Time
The length of time children are concentrating on their play and how many children are involved.
Materials
(a) Which materials are the most popular.
(b) Which materials are never used.
(c) Which materials are always used in the same way.
(d) Which materials lend themselves best to adaptation and improvisation.
(e) Which materials the children combine.
(f) Whether it is always the same group of children that play with the same materials.
(g) When and why the children are destructive with their materials.
Rules
(a) Which rules the children find most difficult to keep.
(b) What rules the children make for themselves.
4 Learning and development:
(a) Emotional.
(b) Social.
(c) Language.
(d) Mathematical.
(e) Scientific.
(f) Physical.
(g) Manipulative.
(h) Problem solving.
(i) Motivation.
(j) Concentration.
(k) Curiosity.

5 Adult's involvement:
   (a) When an adult participated and what she did.
   (b) What an adult initiated.
   (c) Why an adult intervened.

When do I record?

1 If possible at the time when the observation is made. Many teachers find it useful to keep a small 'jotter' handy so that they can note down anything significant as it occurs – it is so easy to forget things in a busy infant room.
2 At the end of the morning or afternoon session.
3 At least once a week: the more often teachers can record the easier it becomes.

How do I record?

1 In a narrative form in a record book kept specially for play.
2 On personally compiled recording sheets for separate categories of play: there are specimen recording sheets on pages 192–4.
3 Using a tape recording for the children's and adult's language at the time of play and for the teacher's subsequent comments.
4 By taking photographs to illustrate the play; these can be used with any of the above methods of recording.
5 By continuous observation.
6 By 'spot checks': during a set period of time while continuing with other classroom activities, the teacher observes what is happening in the play and records her observations later.
7 By setting aside a specific time for either 5 or 6 above at least once a week.
8 By concentrating on each category of play in turn and if possible covering all of these during the course of one term.

Teachers recording on the Project

The Project teachers experimented with methods of recording play. Some used a narrative form and underlined their recordings in a colour code to identify the different kinds of motivation, learning and development, and teacher involvement. This is obviously a lengthy and time-consuming way but the teachers who had the time to follow it found that they had all the information they needed to structure play, and to supplement their records of classroom activities and individual children's profiles.

One group of teachers devised a check sheet but found that this did not give them sufficient detail to use in their structure and that, in order to be comprehensive, it became lengthy and tedious to fill in. A few teachers tried using a flow diagram, but found this took a long time to work out and was too complicated.

The majority of the Project teachers used a recording sheet which we devised and revised with their assistance. As a result of their work we have produced these specimen recording sheets. Sheet 3 incorporates the kinds of comments made by Project teachers at the end of their recording sheet. Experienced teachers who were involved in structuring the play wrote this section of their record in more detail than the previous sections.

We suggest that when teachers become practised in observing, recording and analysing play, they may find sheet 3 provides them with sufficient information on which to base their structure. This shorter form of recording will only be useful to a teacher who is accustomed to structuring play and has already made careful observation of her provision, the children's learning and her involvement.

Specimen sheet for recording play – 1

Category of play: Domestic	Date Friday 16th May	Time 11.00 to 11.30
Names of children involved	John M Phillip S Darren F Mandy H	Susan J Ann P Jennifer T
Space used for play	Carpeted area and corridor.	
Time children concentrated: { Longest: { Shortest:	20 mins 5 mins	
Equipment and materials used most frequently	Table, chairs, bed, doll, pram, hats, lengths of material, handbag, telephone, mirror, shop, cups and saucers.	
Equipment and materials never used	Aprons	
Materials used for improvisation	Lengths of materials for bedclothes and tablecloth. See below.	
Materials imported from another kind of play	Water play tubing for stethoscope, small funnel from sand tray for doctor's medical instrument, polystyrene tube for plaster cast.	
Materials used in a stereotyped way	Telephone. Tables and chairs always used for meal.	
Materials used destructively or aggressively	Wigs	
Rules broken by the children	More than 5 playing house at a time.	
Regulations made by children in course of play	No standing on table or chairs or bed. Girls not allowed to wear peaked hat. Only boys could be doctor, girls give medicine.	
Reason for participation	Went as visitor to invalid to ascertain why she was being examined.	
Reason for intervention	Mandy quarrelling – wanted to be Doctor. Suggested she set up a clinic and be Sister-in-charge and give injections.	
Reason for initiation	Space too crowded – set up clinic by sink so children wanting to play 'illness' didn't obstruct children playing house.	

Specimen sheet for recording play – 2
Examples of learning and development

Emotional	Darren not a 'loner' on this occasion – joined in play as sick child and later became active member going to work with Phillip who was Father serving in shop. Darren served.
Social	At one time 7 children cooperated – 2 in shop, 3 in clinic, 2 in house. Mandy happily being Sister in clinic when disappointed could not be two doctors.
Language	Jennifer talked about a 'pointer' when she meant appointment, corrected by Mandy. Ann as mother showed sympathy for Darren who was ill – 'I'll keep the others quiet while you get some sleep.' Susan said 'littler' yet used word 'responsible' correctly.
Mathematical	Shop accounts kept accurately by Phillip. 5 ml spoonfuls measured by Mandy. 3 minutes timed on 'Pinger' for telephone call – money put in telephone box in house.
Scientific	I offered to show them how to make a telephone from string and cans tomorrow.
Physical	Setting up clinic counter.
Manipulative	Fastening dressing-up clothes. Using improvised instruments.
Problem solving	Need for medical instruments. Counter for clinic made from building bricks and planks.
Motivation	I used clinic play to show children how to organize appointments diary – connected this with their knowledge of time. Darren and Phillip wrote a story about a shopkeeper who was robbed and solved the mystery quicker than the Police.
Drama role playing	Shopkeepers – Invalid – Doctor – Sister – Mother and Father.
Concentration	Mandy – making appointments cards and diary. Susan and Phillip making shop accounts. All groups at varying times during play.
Curiosity	Jennifer didn't know about timing telephone calls – watched Ann and John and then used Pinger herself.

Specimen sheet for recording play – 3

Points to note from this recording to answer the question 'Why do I record play?'

1	What is happening over a period of time?		5th domestic play observation this term. So far play in house confined to meals and illness. Try to interest in other domestic activities. Try to extend clinic play. Wigs still misused, discuss with children which are not needed.
2	Learning development.		Can now include ½p in shop prices, enough children understand halves from maths work. Let Phillip make up new price list. Put up and teach alphabet so that children can make a class telephone directory house in house play. Make time estimation chart for class, put on it How long does it take to? Guess. Now write the correct time here. Use the stop watch.
3	What needs to be added to individual children's records?		Darren now cooperating with Phillip, first time he has played with other children. Phillip's first attempt to write a story, he could add money correctly to £1. Mandy still quarrelsome in a group. Jennifer needs help with clocks and time.
4	Is any action needed?	space	Clear space near sink for clinic as long as play lasts. Put shop nearer house, move display for this space.
		time	Wet day meant no play time. Extra time given to play in house allowed, clinic development. Must try and squeeze extra time for play.
		materials	Provide armchairs, cushions, cleaning materials, water for washing & washing up. Remove some wigs.
		rules	Discuss rule about 6 in house, when can be broken. Discuss need for rule about misuse of house furniture with all class.
5	Is any action needed on teacher's part?	Preparation	Provide materials, book and diagram for home-made telephone. Find hospital books in library.
		Observation	Watch Jennifer, is she too dominated by Susan? Is girl/boy role too stereotyped in house? Would furnishing session help?
		Participation	Join in clinic play to assist Mandy with appointments. Does she need a secretary?
		Initiation	Shall I initiate house furnishing & bringing dolls to Baby Clinic, and discussion about women doctors and male nurses.
		Intervention	Suggest clinic secretary, and Mandy for doctor.

10 Thinking about play

In this chapter we draw together all the points relating to structuring play that have been developed in this book.

The following questions and answers will help teachers to examine their own principles and practice in play. They can be used by individual teachers in their own classrooms, but much more benefit can be derived from them if they are used by more than one teacher for discussion: this may be in a cooperative teaching situation, in a school at a staff meeting or by a group at a teachers' centre. The 'answers' given under Observation and Structuring are some of the points raised during the Project. There will be many that can be added by other teachers. Finally, there are questions which are left for each teacher to answer in order to take a fresh look at the play in her own classroom and pinpoint her own ideas.

Questions and answers on observation and structuring

OBSERVATION

As we said in Part 1, before the teacher can structure play she must observe; only then can she provide, participate, initiate and intervene in the play. Observation is a continuous process which is the basis of all the teacher's involvement.

Why are we observing?
1 To discover what is the children's spontaneous play.
2 To take our cues from the children.
3 To identify which materials are in frequent use.
4 To identify which materials are never used.
5 To discover whether adequate space for play is provided.
6 To discover whether sufficient time for play is allocated.
7 To identify any children who do not play.
8 To identify the children who always play with the same materials.

9   To discover if the play of any children in the class is always repetitive.
10   To identify individual children's difficulties and advantages.
11   To identify learning and development that is occurring.
12   To identify learning and development that could occur.
13   To discover if the teacher needs to be involved in the play more than she is.
14   To identify reasons and time for participating, initiating, intervening.
15   To identify items for record keeping.

What do we observe?
1   The children's spontaneous play.
2   The children's attempts to extend or alter the space allocated for certain types of play.
3   The way in which the time allowed for play structures the children's play and opportunities.
4   The way in which the play materials and opportunities provided promote or restrict the children's learning and development.

When do we observe?
1   Incidentally as often as possible.
2   At set times.
3   At least once a week.
4   When unusual play occurs.

How do we observe?
1   By standing or sitting near to the play to listen to the dialogue and, if the children are disturbed by our interest, appearing to be engaged in some other ploy. When children become accustomed to this interest it does not inhibit their play.
2   By participating in the play.
3   By playing alongside the children.

The teacher has observed, now she is able to structure.

PROVISION

Why are we providing?
1   To give children space to develop and extend play.
2   To give children time to develop and extend play.
3   To give children opportunities to explore materials, environment, situations.

4 To give children opportunities to develop make/believe situations.
5 To give children opportunities to develop role play.
6 To give children opportunities to develop concentration.
7 To give children incentive to observe carefully.
8 To give children opportunities to learn and develop.
9 To give children motivation to learn.

What are we providing?

1 Space.
2 Time.
3 Materials, both manufactured and improvised.
4 Rules.
5 Adult interest and encouragement.
6 Stimulus to observe their environment.
7 Stimulus from pictures, discussion, literature, television.
8 Knowledge and skill.

When are we providing?

1 Throughout the day, no restriction on time.
2 At set times in a day or week which children are aware of.
3 At specified times that can be extended if play needs to continue.

How are we providing?

1 By providing the ordered framework within which children play safely and happily.
2 By dispensing with a table and chair for every child, or other unnecessary furniture, to provide space.
3 By allowing varying lengths of time for the children's play to develop.
4 By organizing the storing of equipment.
5 By regulating or not regulating the number of children able to play at a given time with specified materials or equipment.
6 By periodically reviewing with the children the rules relating to play.

PARTICIPATION

Why are we participating?

1 To show children that adults value play.
2 To share children's enjoyment.
3 To establish a relationship with insecure children.
4 To encourage children who do not know how to play.

5 To develop children's imagination in play situations.
6 To foster children's language.
7 To discover what are their problems in play.
8 To help children solve their problems.
9 To enable an adult to initiate play naturally.
10 To identify where children can be motivated to use skills in their play.
11 To identify where play can be extended into other infant school activities.

When do we participate?
1 As often as we can find time.
2 When children are obviously bored with their play.
3 When play has been repetitive for a considerable time.
4 When we wish to show one or more children how to play.
5 When invited by children to join in play.

How are we participating?
1 As an adult, i.e. not pretending to be a child.
2 As an equal participator in play, not the leader or organizer.
3 As an adult who enjoys playing.
4 As an adult who may be asked to make suggestions and give advice.
5 As an adult who will not expect advice and suggestions necessarily to be followed.
6 As a participator who can withdraw from a play situation without disrupting it.
7 As an adult playing alongside the children, not necessarily joining in their play.

INITIATION

Why are we initiating?
1 To ensure that the potential of play as a learning and development process is fulfilled.
2 To enable the children to sustain their play.
3 To show the children how to extend their play by using their observation, reasoning, imagination, new knowledge and skills.
4 To give the children new knowledge and skills to develop their play.
5 To involve the play in other infant school activities.
6 To guide those children who do not know how to play.

What do we initiate?

1 Opportunity to combine materials.
2 Improvisation with play materials.
3 Exploration of play materials.
4 New vocabulary.
5 New dialogue.
6 Careful observation.
7 Recall of experience, observation, stories, television.
8 Reference to books, pictures, diagrams.
9 Realization of need to write, read, measure, weigh, compute.
10 Transference of knowledge.

When do we initiate?

1 Only after careful observation.
2 If a child or group is unable to play.
3 If after initial exploration of new materials or equipment children are obviously at a loss with them or misusing them.
4 If children have been repeating the same play for a long time.
5 If children ask for information, or a skill to be demonstrated, that will enable them to develop their play.
6 If as a result of discussion or questioning or participation it is obvious that the assistance of an adult is required.

How do we initiate?

1 By providing materials, tools and equipment that children need.
2 By providing materials and encouraging children to improvise with them.
3 By helping children to learn how to use the equipment.
4 By helping children to observe more carefully so that they can reproduce situations and experience and use knowledge gained in their play.
5 By helping children to recall their observation, experience and television viewing through discussion or participation.
6 Through stories that will promote play either by giving knowledge or by encouraging imagination.
7 By taking children out of school on visits or expeditions.
8 By providing books, pictures, magazines, diagrams that adults know are pertinent to the children's play.

INTERVENTION

Why are we intervening?

1 To facilitate the play.

2 To ensure that all the children are able to join in play if they wish to.

3 To enable play to exist among other infant school activities and not disrupt classroom organization.

When do we intervene?

1 When children appeal for help.
2 When children are unable to solve their problems themselves.
3 When play is liable to be disrupted.
4 When equipment is being misused.
5 When children are in danger.
6 When children are interfering with other infant school activities, e.g. being unduly noisy, or using too much space or 'rushing around'.
7 When children are unable to resolve their disagreements themselves.
8 As infrequently as possible, i.e. only after children have had time and opportunity to solve their own problems.

How do we intervene?

1 By providing an extension or change of venue.
2 By reorganizing classroom management after discussion with children.
3 By ensuring that all children understand the classroom organization.
4 By establishing the necessary rules for use of equipment and materials, e.g. water; tools for play with wood.
5 By reminding children periodically of rules when using equipment, and of classroom organization, and revising them when necessary.
6 By acting as arbiter in quarrels.
7 By suggesting ways for facilitating the play situation.
8 By participating.
9 By initiating.

Final questions

Finally, teachers may find it helpful to ask themselves the following questions about the play in their classrooms, and to add to this list as a result of their recorded observations. The questions are concerned with both the principles and practice of play. All teachers know how difficult it is to separate these two in the classroom situation, yet how essential it is to ask 'why?'. The questions are grouped to help the practising teacher focus the ideas in this book on to her particular children. Before she attempts to answer them she must ask herself these questions about play:

1 Do I agree that children learn and develop through play?
2 Do I know how they do?
3 Do I agree that play motivates children to learn?
4 Do I know how it does?
5 If I disagree then why do I provide the opportunity for children to play in the classroom?

CHILDREN LEARN AND DEVELOP THROUGH PLAY

1 What opportunities do I provide for play in my classroom?
2 What aspects of learning and development do I provide for in the play in my classroom?
3 Can I identify all the learning and development that takes place in the play?
4 Do I develop the play to extract all the learning that can come out of it?
5 Do I develop the play so that children use and see the purpose in acquiring skills such as reading and writing?
6 Do the children ever fail in play? Should they?
7 For what reasons is play part of my whole teaching programme and integrated into all activities?
8 For what reasons do I make play a separate period in the day?

STRUCTURING PLAY

Space
1 Do I provide sufficient space?
2 Could I make more space?
3 Do I need a table and chair?
4 Does each child need a table and chair?
5 Is every piece of furniture in the classroom used?
6 Is any piece of equipment never used?
7 Could I make more use of the corridor space?
8 Is the outside space being used all the year round?
9 Do I need to reorganize space periodically and to make room for different types of play?

Time
10 Do I allow enough time for play to develop?

11   Do I allow the children to decide how long they want to play?
12   Do I allow enough time for clearing up?

Materials

13   How do I decide what materials to provide for play?
14   Do I keep a balance of improvised and manufactured materials?
15   Do I know which materials are most frequently used by the children?
16   Have I myself used all the materials to discover their potential?
17   Do I let the children combine play materials or do I keep them strictly separated?
18   Do I introduce and withdraw materials when necessary?
19   Do I regularly check all materials for damage and dirt?
20   What is the chief lack in equipment in my classroom?
21   What opportunities for learning and development are there in clearing up?
22   Is the equipment stored so that it can be reached, taken out and put away by children?
23   Do adults still tidy away equipment instead of training the children to do it?
24   Do I appreciate that at least twice each term I need to go over the clearing-up procedure with the children?

Rules

25   What rules do I make for the children's play?
26   Are they all necessary?
27   Do I periodically review them?
28   Do the children recognize the need for rules?
29   Have the children helped to suggest them?

Teacher involvement

30   What are my objectives when I am involved in the children's play?
31   What do I need to know about the children's backgrounds and home environment in order to provide for play?
32   When do I take time to observe what the children are doing?
33   When did I last take my cues from the children?
34   Do I leave the children sufficient time to play on their own, make their own explorations, solve their own problems and learn social cooperation?
35   How do I judge children's play to be aimlessly repetitive?

36 What do I do when the children's play becomes aimlessly repetitive?
37 When did I last participate in the children's play?
38 How did I last initiate the children's play?
39 Why did I last intervene in the children's play?
40 What stimuli have I used to encourage the play?
41 How do the children know I value their play?
42 Why have I adopted the form of record keeping for play that I use?
43 What use do I make of my records of children's play?

Appendix 1

Domestic Play
Analysis of play on pages 54–5.

Analysis of play on pages 54–5.

HOUSE FURNISHING AND DECORATING

Examples of motivation, learning and development that may occur in this play

1　Emotional role-playing.
2　Cooperation in sharing the effort.
3　Language. The children use language for reasoning when they make or furnish the house: 'I can see out of the window when I'm standing up now. It was too low before, I had to kneel down.'

They report on their actions and recall their first-hand experiences: 'I'm putting the paper on like this. My dad says if you don't stick it on well at the top it falls down and you get yourself stuck up in it.'

They use language to help them imagine situations: 'Would you like a drink from my cocktail cabinet?'

They direct the actions of their companions in the play: 'Please hold this for me someone. I need more hands, that end's coming off.'

They maintain their position in the group: 'Hey, leave that alone – I'm the electrician, I'm seeing to the lights circuit.'

Language is needed to predict the course of events: 'I'm not going to make this cupboard any bigger because if I do it won't go through the door.'

The children use language to project into the reactions of others: 'We have to put newspaper on the floor because Mr T gets very cross if we don't. Paint on the floor makes a lot of hard work for him.'

4 New vocabulary needed: soft furnishings, adhesive, water repellent, gloss, eggshell finish, enamel, diamond hard, bathroom suite, cocktail/kitchen cabinet, period/contemporary furniture, antique, upholster.

5 Mathematical in measuring, matching and estimating.

6 Scientific concepts: balance, stress, strain.

7 Manipulative skill in using tools.

8 Physical skill: lifting and holding boxes and wood, wallpapering.

9 Reading and writing, consulting and making books.

10 Motivation to observe carefully.

11 Motivation for pattern-making and fabric printing.

12 The satisfaction of completing a task successfully.

Analysis of play on pages 56–7.

HOSPITAL PLAY

Examples of motivation, learning and development that may occur in this play

1 Emotional: allaying possible fear or unpleasant experience in role play.

2 Social: cooperation involved in the play, opportunity to be patient or doctor, to boss and be bossed.

3 Shared interests with adults.

4 Language. The children use language in many different ways. They reason: 'She doesn't want a cup of tea now. She's going to sleep because she's just had her injection.'

They recall past experiences as they report on their actions: 'I'm putting this sticky plaster on so's the tube won't fall off. Last time I forgot and Sibesa couldn't keep it on. It wasn't a proper transfusion.'

They use language to express their imagination: 'Your mummy will come to see you at visiting time tomorrow. I expect she'll bring you a present if you're good.'

They direct each other: 'Take your shoes off and stand on the scales. I'm going to weigh you now.'

Their position is maintained through language: 'I have to set the drip up. I'm the Sister. You're only a nurse, nurses aren't allowed to do it.'

They predict the result of actions: 'If you stay in bed you'll soon get better.'

There are many opportunities to project into the reactions of others: 'Are you worried about your little girl? Would you like to have the telephone to talk to her?'

5 New vocabulary needed: ward, surgery, intensive care unit, casualty department, thermometer, syringe, stethoscope, capsules, phial, anaesthetic, antibiotic, disinfectant, sterile dressing, gauze, prescription, five milligrammes, transfusion, blood donor, cubicle.

6 Mathematical concepts: weighing and timing.

7 Scientific concepts involved in being healthy and being ill, in sterile dressings, disinfecting.

8 Manipulative skill in using instruments, bandaging.

9 Physical skill in bed-making.

10 Motivation to observe on visits to a clinic and doctor's surgery.

11 Motivation to observe accurately when television and films portray hospitals.

12 Motivation to refer to books, magazines and pictures.

13 Motivation to read and write.

14 Imagination and initiation involved in devising situations and role play.

15 Concentration and application in sustaining the play.

Construction Play
Analysis of play on pages 79–80.

A TELEVISION PROGRAMME

Examples of motivation, learning and development that occurred in this play

1 Cooperation in building and playing Colditz game.

2 Sharing an experience, i.e. television programme with peers and adults, and solving their misunderstandings of the programme.

3 Language. The children used language for reasoning when they engineered their escapes and constructed the prison: 'Don't make a tunnel there because you'll come out here by the wall and you can't escape that way.'

They reported as they built and drew: 'He's digging a hole under his bed and then he's going to crawl down and when he comes up here he's on the other side of the wall. See.'

They imagined they were the tunnellers and talked as they imagined: 'I don't like being in the dark for a long time like this, do you?'

They directed others: 'Don't put that on there you silly twit. It'll crash them all down.'

They predicted what the result of their actions would be: 'If I don't hurry up the guard will be round again and capture me.'

They projected into the reactions of the prisoners: 'He's terrified they'll find him. He's trying not to cough.'

4 New vocabulary needed: petrified with fright, unsympathetic, fearful, anxious, turret, shackles, observation tower, shore up, moat, dungeon. (It became clear in the discussion that although a grenade had been referred to many times in the last television programme viewed, none of the children knew what it was.)

5 Manipulative skill in fixing interlocking bricks.

6 Physical skill in making escape exits and silently extricating themselves.

7 Problem solving in constructing the prison and devising escape methods.

8 Motivation to observe a programme carefully in order to play and talk about it.

9 Opportunity to dramatize and perhaps minimize the fears caused by a programme.

10 Concentration and application resulting from the interest and vividness of the play.

HOW DID THE TEACHER STRUCTURE THIS PLAY?

1 By providing:

(a) space for this construction. A large space was necessary and the first construction was made on the carpeted area where the children were accustomed to use the bricks. The teacher intervened with another group of children to arrange that the house fixture could be incorporated into the brick play. The children using the house removed their play to the carpeted area. The 'house' was a wooden frame that could be used for a shop, lookout, or small climbing frame as well as for domestic play.

(b) time; these children should have been called away to read to the teacher. When she observed how absorbed they were in their play she did not interrupt on this occasion. Instead she used the reading that resulted from their reference to books and pictures of castles and prisons.

(c) time; the opportunity for the play to continue as long as interest in the television series remained. The play was maintained for the duration of the series: the children were obviously allowed to view each week at home. The teacher followed the series too!

(d) materials for building. Numbers of large bricks were needed to build the wall high enough for the children's purpose.

(e) materials for reading, writing and drawing.

(f) experience of construction, e.g. a high and solid wall. The children had previously worked out with the teacher how to bond bricks and why this was necessary.

(g) the opportunity to destroy a building. The building was reconstructed after each escape and each escape route necessitated some destruction and rebuilding.

2 By involvement.

How did the teacher become involved?

1 By observing the play to identify if involvement was necessary.

2 By participating in the children's play.

3 By intervening. She worked out with the children possible solutions to their problems of escape through recall of the television incidents, and explained any misunderstandings. She encouraged them to try them out in their own construction.

4 By initiating the removal to the house play area, to encourage inventiveness in the use of materials.

5 By showing her own interest in the children's play.

Why did the teacher become involved?

1 Because they did not know what to do once they had built the walls as high as the tallest child.
   Objective: to give the children information that would enable them to solve their problem.

2 Because the children were becoming frustrated at their failure to effect escape routes from the first insecure construction.
   Objective: to give them information that would relieve their frustration, enable them to sustain their interest in the play, and assist them in future construction play. To increase their knowledge of building by showing them how to strengthen their construction.

3 Because she saw the possibilities in the play to foster the children's language, e.g. to discuss the possible feelings of the guards and the prisoners, to describe accurately what they had observed, to predict the outcome of their attempts to escape.
   Objective: to foster the children's language development.

4 Because it was obvious that this play interested the children and could be the motivation for reading, writing, measuring and

scientific activity.

Objective: to extend the play with reading, writing, measuring and science.

5 Because she saw the social and emotional value of the play for the children. They were sharing a common interest in their television viewing which she could enter into, thus combining home and school experience. The play necessitated social interaction both in the building, the planning of the escape routes and the dramatic play that ensued. The children were able to reveal and resolve any fears that the television might have caused. They were able to imagine the feelings of the prisoners and the guards.

Objective: to extend the imaginative potential of this play situation.

Make/Believe Play

Analysis of play on pages 114–16.

A WEDDING

Examples of motivation, learning and development that occurred in this play

1 The group learned how to cooperate and how to organize their making and pretending. They had different leaders at different times. Susan was the leader in the dressing-up sequences because she had been a bridesmaid; Philip was the chief manufacturer of the wedding cake; Claire, who was the mother in the house play, supervised the setting of the wedding reception table and arranged place names. Jeffrey, who had the idea about the straws, took over the top hat construction and all the girls shared in the decorating of the head-dresses and making the bouquets and button-holes.

2 Language was fostered. In discussions the children had to recall and describe events, explain their difficulties, predict the results of their actions.

3 New vocabulary was needed, e.g. celebration, surplice, ceremony, reception, bridegroom, two-tiered.

4 In the make-believe situations they had to enter into the role they were playing, and use appropriate language.

5 Understanding of shape and size was needed to make the top hat and the head-dresses and to cover the wedding-cake tins.

6 Weighing and measuring were needed for making the jellies and cakes.

7 The class became interested in comparing head sizes and built up a histogram.

8 Illustrations in magazines and books were examined carefully and children had practice in observing detail.

9 Problems were solved: the flower stalks, the hat brim, the cake-tiers, covering the wedding-cake boxes.

10 Manipulative skill and hand and eye coordination were improved, especially in fastening a variety of clothes, e.g. buttons, zips, press-studs, hooks and eyes, tying bows.

11 Reading and writing were practised: place cards, invitations, cake boxes were addressed.

12 Motivation to draw, paint, make books occurred. (Some girls painted elaborate pictures of Princess Anne and wedding dresses; one boy painted a picture of soldiers, horse-guards and a royal procession.)

13 Perseverance and concentration produced results which the children could enjoy: cakes and jellies to eat, clothes to wear, parcels to post, books to put in the library and wedding cards to sell in the shop.

HOW DID THE TEACHER STRUCTURE THIS PLAY?

1 By providing:

(a) space inside the classroom and the corridor.

(b) time for the play to continue from morning to afternoon during several days.

(c) time at the end of play for materials and equipment to be tidied away, with either Mrs S or the welfare assistant helping the children when necessary. These children were five year olds and needed to be checked more frequently than older groups that they had tidied materials.

(d) a welfare assistant whose time was organized so that she was free to assist the group when required.

(e) materials; the dressing-up clothes in her room lent themselves to improvisation, e.g. lengths of curtain net for veils and trains, a variety of hats and headgear, attractive sashes and drapes, a full-length mirror fastened to the clothes rack, shoes in an accessible shoe bag holder. These clothes were easily selected and kept uncreased and tidy on coat hangers in a rack. They were frequently washed, ironed or renewed, always on display and therefore encouraged make-believe play.

(f) scrap and collage materials which were stored so that they were readily available and the children knew where to find them. Children were able to help themselves and understood the rules for using scissors, paste and glue. They also knew how to wash utensils and tools and where to store them. No frustration was caused through materials being difficult to find or untangle, or by tools which needed preparing or cleaning before they could be used.

(g) new materials at intervals that she expected would stimulate new ideas, e.g. silver doilies, a cake box, a wedding photograph, an invitation card.

(h) a classroom so organized that children could pass easily from one activity to another, e.g. from making or pretending to writing, without mixing materials and equipment; glue and paint not being used near the dressing-up clothes area.

(i) fresh stimulus as the play progressed and encouragement for the children to bring materials from home.

2 By involvement.

How did the teacher become involved?

1 The children involved Mrs S at the beginning of their play when they told her what roles they had adopted.

2 She talked with them on the second morning to show that her interest, like theirs, was continuing. In this way she discovered what knowledge they had, and what part of the wedding play they were most interested in at this stage. When she knew what suggestions were most likely to fit in with their ideas, she took her cue from the children and discussed wedding clothes and finery.

3 She concentrated on flower posies and buttonholes and head-dresses, which she knew they would be able to make.

4 She made a suggestion in her discussion with the children because she knew that their requirements could be met – tissue paper and beads to make head-dresses and bouquets.

5 She ensured that a new skill was demonstrated when the need arose, e.g. how to measure head-dresses, how to fasten the centre and brim of the top hat.

6 She helped the children when they needed to read, write, count and measure.

7 She examined magazines and pictures with the children, encouraging them to notice details which they might imitate.

8 In her discussions with the children, Mrs S encouraged them

to recall their own experiences and to describe them as accurately as possible so that their play could be developed.

9 She told a larger group of children the story of Rumpelstiltskin, dwelling on the wedding and drawing attention to the illustrations.

10 She brought a book with illustrations of Princess Anne's wedding and told the children the story of how, when she was a little girl, she had been to see the Queen's wedding dress. In this way she maintained the children's interest.

11 She encouraged the discussion about the wedding reception because she knew the children could incorporate cooking into their play.

12 When the children made a pretend wedding cake, she offered the ingredients and recipe for real food. She was uncertain whether this would clash with the pretend cake and wanted to find out what would happen. She expected either that the bride would demand a real cake or that the offer to make jellies and cornflake cakes would be rejected. In the event the children were pleased to make and eat the jellies and small cakes and keep the pretend cake as a decoration on a separate table.

Why did the teacher become involved?

1 Because she observed that the play continued from one day to the next, and that the group had increased. She concluded that the children were genuinely interested and had sufficient knowledge to build on.

2 Because it was obvious after the preliminary discussion that there were not sufficient props on the dressing rack to fulfil the children's needs.

3 Because she thought this was an opportunity to initiate the making of properties for imaginative play situations by the children.

4 Because she wanted to encourage this group of children to persevere in their play with scrap materials and experience the satisfaction of completing and using what they made. She foresaw that the props needed for the wedding play were within the children's ability to make, and yet were sufficiently difficult to pose problems, give rise to ingenuity and demand concentration.

5 Because she believed that their knowledge and interest would sustain the play and that the group would enjoy extending the play if suggestions were made and opportunities given to develop them. She hoped this would give them ideas for extending other

play situations, e.g. cooking and parties in domestic play, making props for role play.

6   Because she knew that it was an interest that would be familiar to many children in the class and that the materials required could be easily provided by school and home.
7   Because these five year olds were beginning to read and write, and she saw many reasons why the children might need to read and write in this play.
8   Because there would be opportunities to promote discussion with the children, encourage dialogue, increase vocabulary and foster language.

What was the result of the teacher's involvement?

1   The children knew that Mrs S was interested in their play and would help them if they needed assistance.
2   The other children and adults in the school became aware of the play and gave encouragement.
3   The play continued over several days.
4   Making and pretending were equally part of the play and continued throughout.
5   The initial situation was extended – to a feast, and wedding-cake posting, later to wedding photographs.
6   The group had to make decisions about the allocation of tasks and organize their time.
7   Satisfaction was gained when props were completed and used.
8   Real cooking became incorporated into the play, the children needed to read a recipe, follow instructions and measure accurately.
9   Reading and writing were introduced into the play: invitations, place names, addresses on the wedding-cake boxes.
10   The children were encouraged to make books.
11   Adult involvement had fostered language.
12   Concentration and perseverance were required.
13   Home and school combined to foster the play.

Appendix 2

Further reading
The books we suggest here are those that we have personally enjoyed reading. Some have also been suggested to us by teachers involved in the Project. We have tried not to overwhelm teachers with a long list of theoretical books and articles on play that are not directly relevant to their work. We include a few books on specialist subjects that are relevant to infant teaching.

Teachers will be familiar with many of the books, but we hope that they will find some that are new to them, and be spurred into re-reading some they have not thought about since their initial training.

Play
The books mentioned in the text are all essential reading and we amplify these further in this list.

A collection of up to date accounts of research and papers on play, generally in readable form, are in:

BRUNER, J. S., JOLLY, A. and SYLVA, K. (Eds) (1976) *Play: Its Role in Development and Evolution* Penguin
HERRON, R. E. and SUTTON-SMITH, B. (Eds) (1971) *Child's Play* Wiley
PIERS, M. (Ed) (1972) *Play and Development* New York: Norton and Company

Modern accounts of play can be found in:

CASS, J. (1971) *The Significance of Children's Play* Batsford
McLELLAN, J. (1970) *The Question of Play* Pergamon
MILLAR, S. (1968) *The Psychology of Play* Penguin
WINNICOTT, D. W. (1971) *Playing and Reality* Penguin

For a philosophical discussion on play:

DEARDEN, R. F. (1967) 'The concept of play' in R. S. Peters (Ed) *The Concept of Education* Routledge and Kegan Paul
DEARDEN, R. F. (1968) *The Philosophy of Primary Education* Routledge and Kegan Paul
HUIZINGA, J. (1949) *Homo Ludens* Routledge and Kegan Paul

'CLASSIC' BOOKS ON PLAY
Although written more than twenty years ago these books are still relevant to play today:

BUHLER, C. (1935) *From Birth to Maturity* Routledge and Kegan Paul
GRIFFITHS, R. (1935) *Imagination in Early Childhood* Routledge and Kegan Paul
HARTLEY, R. E., FRANK, L. K. and GOLDENSON, R. M. (1952) *Understanding Children's Play* Routledge and Kegan Paul
LOWENFELD, M. (1935) *Play in Childhood* Gollancz

Learning and development
To look at play in the overall development of children, teachers could read the books listed in the references in Part 1. In addition we recommend:

DAVIE, R., BUTLER, N. and GOLDSTEIN, H. (1972). *From Birth to Seven* Longman
GESELL, A. M. D. and ILG, F. L. (1965) *The Child from 5–10* Hamish Hamilton

Language
LURIA, A. R. (1959) *Speech and the Development of Mental Processes in the Child* Staples Press
TOUGH, J. (1976) *Listening to Children Talking* Ward Lock Educational
WILKINSON, A. (1971) *The Foundations of Language* Oxford University Press

Mathematics and science
NUFFIELD FOUNDATION (1967 onwards) *Mathematics Project* Chambers and John Murray
LOVELL, K. (1961) *The Growth of Basic Scientific and Mathematical Concepts* University of London Press

Schools Council (1972, fourth edition) *Mathematics in Primary Schools* (Curriculum Bulletin No. 1) HMSO
Schools Council (1974) *Science 5–13* Macdonald Education

Art and crafts
Plaskow, D. (1968) *Art with Children* Studio Vista
Pluckrose, H. (1966) *Creative Arts and Crafts* Oldbourne
Pluckrose, H. (1969) *Creative Themes* Evans
Sparkes, R. (1975) *Exploring Materials with Young Children* Batsford

Organization
Dean, J. (1972) *Room to Learn Series: Working Space; A Place to Paint; Language Areas* Evans
Douet, K. *et al* (1975) *Working an Integrated Day* Ward Lock Educational
Rance, P. (1971) *Record Keeping in the Progressive Primary School* Ward Lock Educational
Ridgway, L. and Lawton, I. (1968) *Family Grouping in the Primary School* Ward Lock Educational
Taylor, J. (1971) *Organizing and Integrating the Infant Day* Allen and Unwin

'Fun' books!
Finally we list books which we find great fun to read as well as subscribing to our knowledge of play:

Axline, V. (1971) *Dibs: In Search of Self* Penguin
Caldwell Cook, H. (1917) *The Play Way* Heinemann
Chukovsky, K. (1968) *From Two to Five* Cambridge University Press
Stevenson, R. L. (1963) 'Child's Play' in *Virginibus Puerisque and Familiar Studies of Men and Books* Dent

Appendix 3

How to use *Structuring Play in the Early Years at School*
This book has been written to help teachers develop play in school. Teachers who wish to gain the maximum benefit from the book and develop their own skills in structuring play should work through the analyses, answer the questions posed and try out the ideas suggested in their own classrooms.

Individual teachers can use the book but, as we have described, much more would be gained by groups of teachers working through it together. We think workshop courses extending over two or three terms are the best way to develop skills in structuring play. The Project video-tapes that illustrate each category of play give teachers the opportunity to observe children and analyse play in a way that is not possible in a busy infant classroom. They also provide common examples of play for groups to observe and discuss.

The Project is organizing workshops to train group leaders who will conduct courses within their own areas. If teachers are unable to join a group it may be possible for the staff of a school to work together, using the book and video-tapes.

Teachers could follow the same pattern of work as the Project teachers and focus on each category of play in turn. The length of time and order in which this is done will depend on individual teachers' circumstances. We suggest at least half a term on each category of play, taken in the order they are written in the book:

1 Domestic Play
2 Construction Play
3 Make/Believe Play
4 Play with Natural Materials
5 Play Outdoors.

This will give time for new ideas and materials to be tried out, the play to develop and teachers to build up their own skills in structuring play.

The activities suggested for the categories of play can be carried out over the half-term period and, if meeting together, teachers can bring their recordings to discuss and analyse as a group.

Information about dissemination workshops can be obtained from the Project Directors, Miss Kathleen Manning and Mrs Ann Sharp, The Education Area, The University of Sussex, Brighton.

The video-tapes and accompanying booklet are available from Drake Educational Associates, 212 Whitchurch Road, Cardiff CF4 3XF.

Index

aesthetic 54, 96, 188

caretakers 121, 162, 178
classroom organization 26, 34, 184, 201
   books on 216
   (*see also* clearing up play)
clearing up play 184, 185–7, 202
   outdoors 162, 165
concentration, in play 34, 49, 54, 102, 197, 210, 212, 213
   motivation for 14, 65, 72, 207
   time for 70, 96, 161, 189
cooperation 62, 64, 75, 79, 105, 110, 135, 139, 152, 153, 171, 174, 204
   by schools 179
   encouraging 74, 97, 112, 121
   home and school 99
   in clearing up 185
   lacking 62
   over a period 102
   social 38 40, 50, 56, 68, 187, 205, 206, 209
coordination 91, 99, 111
cues, taken from the children 8, 17, 18, 32, 34, 57, 86, 202
curiosity 190, 193

dialogue 15, 73, 78, 99, 106, 132, 135, 145, 152, 179, 196
discovery 20, 31, 134, 143, 147, 162
   behaviour of materials 13, 53, 85, 91, 124, 141–3, 145, 151
discussion
   in Construction Play 63–8, 70, 73, 75, 77, 79, 80, 207
   in Domestic Play 37, 39, 40, 43, 47, 48, 50, 52
   in Make/Believe Play 97, 98, 101, 105–7, 109, 112–14, 209, 211–13
   in Play Outdoors 168, 174
   in Play with Natural Materials 129, 132, 139, 143, 146, 148, 151, 152, 154, 155
   in the classroom 14, 16, 18, 23, 187
   when carrying out Project's ideas 9, 33, 34, 57, 121, 195, 199, 200, 217, 218
drawing 14, 66, 67, 72, 79, 90, 98, 99, 143
   and imagining 85, 92, 95
   cooperating in 96
   motivation for 41, 46
dressing up 14
   in Construction Play 71, 73
   in Domestic Play 39, 46, 48, 52
   in Make/Believe Play 29, 85–9, 101, 106, 115–17, 209–11
   in Play Outdoors 167, 173

emotional development 13, 18, 30, 31, 38, 74, 91, 163, 189, 193, 204, 205, 209
enjoyment 14, 15, 21, 22, 34